THE HISTORY OF
SUTTON COLDFIELD
MUNICIPAL CHARITIES

THE HISTORY OF
SUTTON COLDFIELD
MUNICIPAL CHARITIES

Donald J. Field

BREWIN BOOKS

First published by
Brewin Books Ltd, 56 Alcester Road,
Studley, Warwickshire B80 7LG in 2011

www.brewinbooks.com

ISBN: 978-1-85858-475-1 (Paperback)
ISBN: 978-1-85858-476-8 (Hardback)

A Cataloguing in Publication Record
for this title is available from the British Library.

Typeset in Minion Pro
Printed in Great Britain by
Hobbs the Printers Ltd.

CONTENTS

ACKNOWLEDGEMENTS

MUCH OF the information contained in this book came from the Minute Books of the Municipal Charities which are now stored in the Reference Library in Sutton Coldfield or in the offices of the Charities in Walmley and I thank the Local Studies Department of Sutton Coldfield Library for allowing me access to the records and for the use of photographs. I am particularly indebted to Marian Baxter, the Local Studies Librarian, for her support and advice and especially for her help in selecting and copying most of the photographs.

I am very grateful to the Trustees of the Sutton Coldfield Municipal Charities who have been very supportive and patient throughout the research and writing and in publishing the finished product. I am particularly grateful to my successors as Clerk to the Trustees, Andrew MacFarlane and Ernie Murray for their help and support. Finally, I warmly thank my wife who put up with an absentee and preoccupied husband who spent a great deal of time poring over large dusty volumes or slowly tapping away at a computer keyboard.

PREFACE

AFTER TRAINING in science and a career in education I was fortunate to be appointed Clerk to the Trustees of Sutton Coldfield Municipal Charities soon after the death of Paul Holden, Ll.B, who had been the holder of the post for thirty one years and also Town Clerk of Sutton Coldfield until 1974 when the borough became part of the City of Birmingham. In the records of the Charities were the notes for several talks which he had given to the Trustees and others about the origins and history of the Charities and also a tape recording of his last talk. During the years after my appointment I began to appreciate the long history of the Charities and how they had evolved over a period approaching five hundred years but information was scattered in many different documents.

Although not a historian I decided that it would be interesting to research the history of the Charities and create a record for future generations. When I retired, with the support of the Trustees, I began to read the literature available and decided fairly quickly that I would concentrate on the period of the Municipal Charities which began soon after the incorporation of Sutton Coldfield by a charter of 1886. I also decided that I would not continue beyond 2000, although in order to complete the account of a few developments there are some references to events after this date of Trustees' meetings.

During the period studied, the minutes of the Trustees' meetings vary in the amount of detail they include, depending on circumstance at the time, and unfortunately the first minute book seems to be missing, but they do provide a fascinating account of the work of the Trustees and their staff and of life at the time. The early ones are handwritten and later ones are typewritten with the most recent ones being produced on a word processor so the quality is somewhat variable.

I hope that this account will be of interest to local people and others interested in charitable activities and add to our knowledge and understanding of some aspects of the life of an ancient town.

Chapter 1

THE EARLY YEARS, AN OVERVIEW

THE ORIGINS of Sutton Coldfield Municipal Charities may be traced back to the reign of Henry VIII and the Charter which established a governing body for the town. In the early part of the sixteenth century it was said that the township of Sutton Coldfield had "fallen into decay, but through the interest of John Vesey *alias* Harman, Bishop of Exeter, a native of the place, Henry VIII was induced on 16th December, 1528 to incorporate the inhabitants, by the name of the Warden and Society of the Royal Town of Sutton Coldfield" (Victoria History of the County of Warwick, vol. IV, Oxford University Press, 1947). The Charter nominated as the first Warden William Gybons (Gibbons), who married the youngest sister of John Harman, to hold office for one year. Male inhabitants "of the age of twenty-two years at the least" were to choose twenty four of their number to form the Society for one year and thereafter they were to meet annually on All Souls Day and choose replacements to fill vacancies caused by retirement or death.

The Charter also identified the duties and responsibilities of the Warden and Society (the Corporation). Those listed in the oath sworn by each member on taking office included "he shall take care that the rent and profits of the lands and tenement, commonly belonging to the Warden and Society, may be yearly distributed, in exoneration of the poor inhabitants within the said lordship ... or for the building of houses within the lordship ... or for the marriage of poor girls, or any pious secular use, and to no other use may be applied or converted." The allowances made for marriage were later referred to as Poor Maidens' Portions and are fully described in Chapter 2 below.

Bishop Vesey made his own contribution to the charities which developed for the benefit of Sutton Coldfield residents with the gift of fifteen acres of land at Wiggins Hill. The income from the mowing of this land, which became known as The Lord's Meadow, was used for the benefit of fifteen widows in the parish. Later there was an exchange of this land with a plot at Hill and this continues to be identified as The Lord's Meadow.

Other local philanthropists also established charities, of which the best known and longest surviving was the Charity of Thomas Jesson which was to provide apprenticeships and tools for poor boys. It survived as a separate charity until 2001. Others were more transient and are described in the next chapter.

Towards the end of the eighteenth century there was considerable dissatisfaction with the management of some of its property by the Corporation and in 1788 a group of townspeople, led by William Twamley made a complaint to the Court of Chancery. They argued that the Corporation had been cutting down timber and selling it below its proper value and that land had been enclosed and then leased out at rents below the correct value. The Court of Chancery granted an injunction which prevented the Corporation from selling any more timber and the proceeds of previous sales were impounded. The case proceeded for something like forty years by which time the sum of money in the hands of the Court had risen to over £40,000 which made possible a major development for the local people.

In 1813, the Rector of Sutton Coldfield, John Riland, persuaded a committee of local people to put together a petition urging that the accumulated funds be used to establish elementary schools and he was supported by the complainants to the Court of Chancery and the headmaster of the grammar school. Approval was granted for the school plans by a Scheme of the Court of Chancery on 14th May 1825 and the Town School opened in the following year. Other schools were built and administered by the Warden and Society. The same Scheme also amalgamated several of the Charities administered by the Corporation into "The Corporation Charity".

As the century progressed and more elected corporations were established under the Municipal Corporations Act the people of Sutton Coldfield were divided about incorporation with petitions being organised on both sides. The matter was settled when "Sir Charles Dilke's Corporation Bill was enacted and those Corporations not appointed by previous Acts were extinguished. This was the end of the road for the Warden and Society" (Jones, D.V., 1973) A new Charter came into force in 1886 and brought to an end the control of Sutton Coldfield by the self-selecting Warden and Society.

With the support of the Warden and Society the Charter provided for an elected Council and divided the borough into six wards each of which elected three Councillors and an Alderman. This new Corporation of twenty four men elected a mayor from among themselves, the first one being Sir Benjamin Stone, who also held the office on five subsequent occasions. The Corporation assumed responsibility for the powers and duties listed in the Municipal Corporations Act 1882 and these covered a range of services but a notable omission was the charitable duties and, importantly, all the property which provided the income for the charitable activities.

A new body, Sutton Coldfield Municipal Charities was set up by a Scheme of 1898 and was administered by a Board of Trustees comprising sixteen members of whom eight were nominated by the new Council and eight were co-opted. The Municipal Charities thus became an independent body except that from time to time the Council nominees were able to exert considerable influence and there were occasions when they co-opted other Councillors to give themselves a majority.

Since then the Municipal Charities have made a very important contribution to the well-being of the inhabitants of Sutton Coldfield through the provision of education, the care of those in need and by contributions to a large range of organisations which provide care and recreation for local people. Towards the end of the twentieth century the income grew and enabled much more to be spent as grants until the Trustees' report for 2008 shows that the income for the year was over £2 million and that, after the payment of management costs, nearly £1.4 million was used to run the almshouses and make grants. After Sutton Coldfield was absorbed into Birmingham in 1974 the Charity Commissioners issued a new Scheme in 1982 which reduced the influence of the Council by creating a Board of twelve Trustees of whom eight were co-opted by fellow Trustees and four were nominated by the City Council. The latter were almost invariably residents of Sutton Coldfield or people with good local knowledge.

The philanthropic work of the Municipal Charities continues to be limited to those who live within the boundaries of the former Borough as they existed in 1974 except for cases when an organisation, such as a special school or a hospital for example, outside those boundaries is the only one able to meet the needs of residents.

So, for approaching five hundred years, the intention of the Charter of Henry VIII to provide for the care of needy residents has been met and adapted as society and its needs have changed. The residents are fortunate to have such a considerable asset available.

Chapter 2

THE CONSTITUENT CHARITIES

WHEN SUTTON Coldfield Municipal Charities was established following the setting up of the Municipal Borough of Sutton Coldfield in 1886 and regulated by a Scheme dated 25th January, 1898, it comprised three charities: The Corporation Charity, later known as the General Charity, which was included in a Scheme approved by the Master of the Court of Chancery on 14th May, 1825, The Lord's Meadow for which no date is recorded and the Charity of Thomas Jesson which was set up in a lease of 25th and 26th April 1707. The Corporation Charity provided almshouses and fulfilled a number of charitable functions, some of which were treated as separate charities. These included Poor Maidens' Portions, the Lying In Charity and the Ladies Charity. In 1953 a new charity was established by the will of Mrs Clara Fowler who was the widow of the former surveyor and it was administered by the Municipal Charity Trustees. This was to provide a widow's pension and to supplement the stipend of the curate at Holy Trinity Parish Church. In 1952, by a new Scheme from the Charity Commissioners, the Trustees assumed responsibility for the Sutton Coldfield Provident Dispensary and the Victoria Jubilee Aid-In-Sickness Fund.

The life of these charities, each of which had quite specific objectives, varied in length but they were all affected by two factors. Where specific amounts of money for grants had been prescribed these became of reducing significance as inflation developed over the years and, secondly, the development of the National Health Service and other aspects of the welfare state reduced the need for charitable assistance. Conversely, towards the end of the twentieth century the dramatically increased income of the Municipal Charities led to a general increase in both the number and size of grants from the General Charity and they outstripped those from the smaller attached charities which are now described.

THE LORD'S MEADOW CHARITY

The earliest reference to the Lord's Meadow occurs in a bailiff's account for 1433 which refers to a meadow called Petymore near Peddimore Hall. (Lea 2003). It was also known locally as the Widow's acre. In 1834 in the very extensive report of the Charity Commissioners they describe:

> "a meadow ... in the quarter called Beyond the Wood and Warmley (sic), known by the name of the Lord's Meadow and containing about 12 acres, which has been beyond memory divided into 15 portions, appropriated to the use of 15 poor widows of the parish".
>
> (Further Report of the Charity Commissioners, 1834)

> "The Commissioners were 'not able to discover any documents explaining the origin of this charity, but it is the tradition of the place that it was derived from the gift of Vesey, Bishop of Exeter'. The widows had the first mowing of hay but the 'aftermath and winter feed' were taken by the farmer next to it and he, in return, kept the fences repaired".
>
> (ibid)

Under the provisions of the Enclosure Act, the Lord's Meadow was given up to the farmer while the Warden and Society, who were the Trustees of the Lord's Meadow, were given instead three parcels of land at Hill Wood owned by Francis B Hacket of Moor Hall. The Warden and Society were to either reimburse Hacket for the trees on the land or to allow him to fell them. In accordance with their wishes, the widows were to continue to take the hay from Peddimore during their lifetimes but their successors were to receive the rents of the land at Hill Wood. In their property schedule, the present Surveyors to the Municipal Charities still refer to this land, which is between Grange Lane and Hillwood Common Road, as the Lord's Meadow but none of the Schemes which have regulated the Charities for over a century use this description in the lists of properties.

In January 1903, because of the large number of applicants three additional ladies were elected to the Lord's Meadow Charity. For fifty years, as the widows ceased to own cattle, the Trustees awarded pensions of £2 a year to them and their number was increased from 15 to 18, as funds were available. When a vacancy occurred due to the demise of one of the widows it was advertised and the Trustees selected a suitable beneficiary from one of the applicants. Until the 1940s the number of applications varied between six and seventeen and there were occasionally up to four vacancies to fill at any one time. One of the most deserving cases was in 1912 when one of the seventeen applicants was a widow aged 67 whose rent was paid by her daughter and who chopped wood for a living. She was bringing up the two children, aged 9 and 12, of another daughter who had died.

The number of applications began to decline so that in 1944, for example, there was only one applicant but three vacancies although a later advertisement produced three applications which were all successful. In 1946 three awards were made, although there were only two vacancies, because there was a surplus of funds but in 1951 there were no applications and again in 1959, when two vacancies occurred, there was no response at first but later in the year four vacancies were filled from four applications. Presumably, by this time an annual pension of £2 was not particularly attractive.

Three years later, the Clerk presented a report to the Trustees in which he reminded them of the history of this Charity and showed that the income was £40. 17. 8 from rent and dividends, expenses amounted to £4 and £36 was being divided between the widows.

He went on to report that an increase in investment income and compensation for the loss of development rights could produce a total of over £110 a year so two vacancies could be advertised. The Trustees decided that they would award eighteen widows the sum of £5 a year each, giving an annual expenditure of £90. Unfortunately, they did not implement this policy and there were few applicants so in January 1963 the Trustees decided not to advertise vacancies until there were only six widows left who would receive £6 a year each but this was not implemented either. By September 1966 the number of widows had fallen to fifteen and there was a balance of £112 in the fund so the Trustees again decided to raise the pension from £2 to £5. A year later there were eight vacancies and in 1968 they decided to advertise another vacancy but by the next year they had reversed this policy, perhaps because of the new Scheme, and decided to review the situation annually. In accordance with the new Scheme, which had been sealed in 1968, the Lord's Meadow Charity, after about 440 years, was subsumed into the General Charity and ceased its separate existence. By 1975 there were six pensioners receiving £8 a year each and the Trustees decided to make no further awards. This is the last reference to the charity and one assumes that the pensions continued until the death of each of the widows.

THE CHARITY OF THOMAS JESSON

Thomas Jesson, who is reputed to have been a silk merchant living in Sutton Coldfield, planned to leave £100 in his will for the benefit of poor people living in the parish but he died before the document was completed. However, his family agreed to carry out his wish and provided the money so that the interest might be used by the churchwardens to help the poor. As there were several other sums of money which had been given for similar purposes and were under the control of the Churchwardens, Richard Scott and Nathaniel Ford, these were added and amounted to a further £25.

In April 1707 these funds were used to purchase:

> "five pieces of land, meadow and pasture grounds, lying in Hill, in the said Parish of Sutton Coldfield, containing by estimation about 15 acres, called the Five Sidalls … upon trust yearly to suffer the rents and profits of the said premises to be received and taken by the churchwardens and overseers of the poor of the parish of Sutton Coldfield … to disburse the yearly sum of 40 shillings as a dole for poor people … on St Thomas's-day."
> (Further Report of the Charity Commissioners, 1834)

Any funds remaining after payment of expenses and this dole were to be used:

> "for the binding of poor children apprentices, whose parents should be poor inhabitants of the said parish of Sutton Cold-field, and should be overburthened with children, and should not receive any parish pay or collection".
>
> (ibid)

The charity was to be administered by John Jesson (Thomas Jesson's uncle and heir), his three sons, George Sacheverell of New Hall, nine residents of Sutton, and the two churchwardens. They were to meet at the parish church on the 21st November between the hours of eleven and one, "at the tolling of the bell" to receive the rents and to allocate the funds. The churchwardens were required to give an annual account of the payments and receipts at a meeting of the Trustees and when the number of Trustees was "by death reduced to three" those remaining were required to hand over to "ten more of the most substantial, honest and discreet inhabitants of the parish" (ibid) and to members of the Jesson family.

In 1834 the Charity Commissioners reported that the trusts had been regularly renewed and the objects met. On average during a six-year period three boys each year had been apprenticed and the accounts had been audited and approved at the meeting on 21st November each year. In 1832 there was a balance of £33 16s 3d. The Commissioners also reported that after the meeting "for the convenience of business", the Trustees adjourned to a public house where they paid their own expenses. This tradition is continued to the present day when, although they do not adjourn to a pub, some of the Trustees have a glass of wine at the end of the meeting.

For the next one hundred years the minutes of the Trustees' meetings show that grants to boys for apprenticeships continued to be made at the rate of three or four each year although occasionally more were awarded. For example, in 1924 all seven applicants were successful and in the following year there were six awards but the exceptional year was 1912 when, despite opposition from some of the Trustees, nine awards were made. Sometimes the records show to which trade the boys were apprenticed. In 1911 there were three to boot makers and one to the blacksmith at Little Sutton. The following year we are told that one of the awards was for "a boy who is deaf and dumb" to become a boot maker and there is a reference in 1930 to an award of £5 to "a crippled boy" for training at the Royal Cripples Hospital as a boot maker. In 1937 an apprentice-ship was cancelled because, after three months trial, "the boy's height is against him and he does not seem to have the adaptability necessary to make a successful tradesman".

The records of the Charities contain very few references to the First World War but in 1914 two apprenticeship deeds were suspended "because the boys are on Military Service". Although there is no record of any discussion about the value of the grants made, it is noted in the minutes that the value of the grants was increased from £5 to £10 in 1917 and in November 1919 there was a special award of £20 for an apprenticeship to the Borough Electrical Engineer for two years. Grants for apprenticeship continued to be made during the Second World War although in May 1941 two apprenticeships were cancelled because "the boys wish to join the forces". In 1945 only one grant for apprenticeship was awarded and there are no further references to apprentice-ships until January 1952 when the Clerk reported to the Trustees that there was a surplus of £783 and that the "functions of this particular part of Jesson's Charity are falling into disuse". Later that year the Charity Commissioners wrote to the effect that the endowments for apprenticing would be placed under the jurisdiction of the Ministry of Education. In 1959 the Clerk wrote a special report for the Trustees about Jesson's Trust in which he stated that apprenticing had "failed by reason of the National Builders Federation being responsible for the apprenticing to the building trade, *the latter being the principal trade of the Borough.*" He also reminded the Trustees that various business firms had their own apprentice schemes. At this time the surplus had risen to over £1,200 and the Ministry of Education was asked to produce a Scheme for its disposal and for Jesson's to become part of the main Charity. Two years later, in February 1961, the new Scheme for "The Foundation of Thomas Jesson for Apprentic-ing" was sealed and this allowed the Trustees to use the income not required for apprenticing for residents of Sutton Coldfield:

> "who at the time of the first grant are not more than 25 years of age, who in the opinion of the Trustees are in need of financial assistance and who are preparing for, entering upon or engaged in, any profession, trade, occupation or service, by the provision of outfits, including books, equipment or necessaries, or by the payment of fees for instruction, travel or maintenance expenses or by such other means for their advancement in life or to enable them to earn their own living, as the Trustees think fit."
>
> (Ministry of Education Scheme, sealed 8th February, 1961)

These new provisions enabled the Trustees to make grants to help with fees for students wishing to attend a variety of courses, including music, drama and, in one case, dentistry, and there were many grants for tools, books, travel costs and other expenses. By 1981 the grants were usually of between £100 and £200 but there were very few for apprenticeships. The new Scheme introduced in 1982, after the merger of Sutton Coldfield with Birmingham, maintained the separate status of the Charity of Thomas Jesson as one of the three constituent charities but instructed the Trustees to apply the income, after the payment of property and administrative expenses, to augmenting the income of the

General Charity. However, separate accounts were still required and this added to the administrative costs of the Charities. In the years following, the distinction between grants made from Jesson's Charity, with its upper age limit of 25 years, and educational grants made from the General Charity became increasingly irrelevant so, when a new Scheme was sealed in June 2001, Jesson's Charity was absorbed totally into the Municipal Charities and, after almost three centuries, ceased to exist.

It will be recalled that the original deed by which Jesson's Charity was established set out another object which was to provide a dole for the poor people of the Parish and although references to this dole are irregular it seems to have been paid annually. In January 1924 there is also mention of a payment of a dole of ten shillings to the Churchwardens and this seems to have been in addition to the Jesson dole. There are no further references to the dole until the Rector, Canon Boggon, wrote to the Clerk in 1947 about the non-payment of doles of ten shillings and £2 since 1937. Intriguingly, one of the Trustees, Mr S D Collins, said he "would submit certain particulars to the Clerk affecting this Trust" and at the next meeting the Clerk reported on correspondence with Mr Collins, although the content is not recorded in the minutes, but the Clerk then wrote a report which was attached. After a learned discourse on the precise wording of the original deed in which he explored various legal arguments he came to the view that the dole was not "legally payable to the Church Wardens and should be administered by the Trustees as a dole for the poor of the Parish of Sutton Coldfield". He also revealed that payments had stopped in 1937 at the request of a former Rector. There is no record of any decision being taken following this report but in a later one (January 1952) the Clerk told the Trustees that the dole was discontinued in October 1947.

In 1952 the Charity Commissioners, who were in conflict with the Trustees about proposed almshouse improvements, also became concerned about Jesson's Charity and insisted that the dole be paid by apportioning the assets between the dole provision for which they were responsible and the apprenticing provisions controlled by the Ministry of education. They also insisted that the Trustees must credit the poor with £2 "for any year for which no money has been applied for this purpose and to inform the Charity Commissioners accordingly." The Clerk was instructed to make further enquiries and a few months later he reported there was a balance of almost £860 and that as no payment had been made since 1937, £30 was due to be credited for the benefit of the poor. The Commissioners were asked to allow some of the balance to be used for the non-educational charity but they replied that jurisdiction over the apprenticing part of the charity was now with the Minister of Education so the balance had to be apportioned between the poor and apprenticing.

As there are no more references to the dole we must assume that the back payment was credited to the General Charity but by this time an annual sum of £2 would have been negligible compared to its other resources and the allocations fell into disuse. The dole certainly ceased to exist when the 1982 Scheme was sealed.

In 2002, during a search of the archives, thirty two dole books in the name of Thomas Jesson were discovered for the years 1701 to 1707 and then 1748 to 1777. These books, one for each year, show doles paid to residents in the following quarters: Great Sutton, Hill Hook, Little Sutton, Moore and Ashfurlong, Maney and the Wild, and Walmley and Beyond the Wood. In 1834 the Charity Commissioners recorded the St Thomas Day payments by the Church wardens as follows:

	£. s. d.
Thomas Jesson's	2. 0. 0
Addye's	2. 0. 0 (1762)
V. Sachheverell's	1. 0. 0
Sedgwick's	3. 0. 0 (1665)
Corporation	0. 18. 0 (this payment is shown as 16s in the text)
Anonymous	0. 13. 6
	9. 13. 6 (this is the total shown in the report)

Earlier in the report the Commissioners also refer to bequests from Nicholas Dolphin, Mary Jenks (1750) and William Blakesley (1803) which, together with Valen Satcheverell's charity, form part of a total of £90 deposited in "the savings bank at Sutton Coldfield" which produces £3. 4s 0d for distribution on St Thomas Day.

In April 1986 the Rector of Sutton Coldfield wrote to the Trustees asking the Municipal Charities to accept "certain charities administered by the Church". These were later revealed to be the charities of:

George and Valens Sacheverell, capital £88, for the poor of
the Parish, circa 1715.

> Sedgwick, capital £45, for the poor of Sutton Coldfield circa
> 1665.
> Cup Dole capital £5 for poor persons
> Thomas Cooper, circa 1687
> John Addye, apprenticing poor children and help for the
> poor.

The Trustees replied that they were willing "on receipt of full details from the Rector" and that they would become part of the General Charity and not kept separate. There is no evidence that the transaction took place and a long-serving Trustee informed the writer that it did not.

THE LYING IN CHARITY

The Charter of Henry VIII did not identify specific ways in which the Warden and Society were to allocate funds for the relief of the poor but in 1825 the Court of Chancery approved a scheme which set out in some detail some of the ways in which charitable funds were to be used. (Riland Bedford 1891, Charity Commissioners 1834). Two forms of aid specifically mentioned were described by the Commissioners as follows:

> "For medical assistance, vaccination of the poor inhabitants gratis, attending poor married women in child-bed in their own houses, £31. 10s per annum."
> "Poor married women should be supplied with sheets and child-bed linen to be lent to them during their confinement, for which there should be allowed annually £35."

From 1896 onwards there are references to "The Lying In Charity" although there does not seem to have been a scheme setting up a separate charity and it was part of the Corporation Charity, but later there are also references to "the Ladies Charity" and the "Lady's Committee". The latter comprised educated and prominent ladies, some of whom were the wives and daughters of members of the Corporation. They made recommendations and took an active part in charitable work. In 1901 the Trustees received separate accounts from "Sutton Coldfield Ladies Charity" and the Lying In Charity. The former showed payments for doctors' fees, £5 to Mrs Deeks and clothing to relieve twenty one cases.

The accounts of the Lying In Charity also showed payments to the doctor (£16), Mrs Deeks (£5), clothing and shawls (£5) and one grant of £1. Perhaps these two charities dealt with the two objectives above.

As there is no further mention of the Ladies Committee after 1901 it was presumably either discontinued or subsumed into the Lying In Charity (See below). The accounts for the following year show exactly the same expenditure and similar accounts were submitted annually. Each year the Trustees made grants, usually of £35 to top up the funds available for this charity. It was administered by a committee of ladies who were the wives or sisters of prominent citizens, many of them Councillors or Trustees, and by 1907 there were twenty of them, with a sub-committee of three who presumably considered individual applications. The rules for the administration of the charity were quite stringent and are set out below.

Although the minutes of the board meetings for the Municipal Charities do not record either the Lying In Charity accounts or a grant to it each year, payments seem to have continued. Where there are records, the grant was usually the £35 set out by the Chancery scheme but in one year it was only £15 and in another there was no grant at all because of the balance left from previous years.

In 1900 the Trustees held a special meeting to discuss an application to the Charity Commissioners for a new scheme to regulate the Municipal Charities and their proposals included the abolition of the Lying In Charity. However, when a new scheme was eventually sealed on 23rd June, 1905 one of the yearly payments required by it was:

> "A sum of not more than £35 for the benefit of deserving and necessitous women resident in the said borough at the time of their confinement, such sum to be paid either directly by the Trustees to the beneficiaries or to a Maternity Society or other like association."

In 1923, the Charities Committee of the Municipal Charities reported to the Board that "they have received the books and papers of the Lying In Charity, the committee administering same having decided to disband, and your committee have decided to consider the question of the continuance of this charity at their next meeting." Presumably they did but there is no further reference to the matter until 1927 when the Clerk reported that bags of linen formerly used by the Lying In Charity were to be handed over to the Maternity and Child Welfare Committee. Apparently, the need for this charitable support had been superseded by local health provision and, despite the requirements of the Charity Commissioners in the 1905 scheme, no further grants to assist women in childbirth seem to have been made and that was the end of the Lying In Charity.

THE SUTTON COLDFIELD PROVIDENT DISPENSARY

After the setting up of the National Health Service the assets of the Dispensary, which was also known as the Victoria Jubilee Dispensary, were handed over to the Municipal Charities in October 1948 and in 1952 the building was sold and the proceeds temporarily invested in a separate bank account.

In March of that year the Commissioners sealed a Scheme which decreed that the Trustees were to apply the yearly income "for the benefit of sick persons" in the following ways:

1. The supply of special food, medical comforts, extra bedding, fuel and medical and surgical devices.
2. Provision of domestic help.
3. A grant of money to purchase as in 1. or to defray the expenses of convalescence or domestic help during convalescence.

But there was to be no relief of rates, taxes or other public funds and no periodical or recurrent benefit.

This new charity was to be known as the Victoria Aid-In-Sickness Fund and its assets comprised 206 square yards of land on the corner of Coleshill Street and Rectory Road, shares to the value of £2,378 and £510 in a bank account (Charity Commission Scheme sealed 14.3.1952).

THE VICTORIA JUBILEE AID-IN-SICKNESS FUND

In September 1953 the money was invested in Corporation Stock and the benefits from the fund were published to the local doctors, clergy and to the general public. A subcommittee, comprising the Chairman of the Board, the Chairmen of the two committees and Rev. Boggon (Rector of Sutton Coldfield and a Trustee) was established to consider applications and make awards.

In July 1954 the Trustees decided to advertise the Fund and also made eleven awards which included grants for bed linen, special food, coal, Horlicks (sic), blankets and payments for home help. In subsequent years a sub-committee of Rev. Boggon, Mr S D Collins and Ald. F W Terry were given executive powers to make grants and they dealt with three to ten applicants each time, meeting about twice a year. Most of the awards were for coal but there were also grants for bedding, shoes, bath seats and a child's convalescence together with occasional awards of money. No reasons are given but in 1967 the Trustees made a successful application to the Charity Commissioners for this fund to be amalgamated with the General Charity.

CLARA FOWLER

About two weeks before she died on the 18th May, 1935, the widow of the former surveyor to the Municipal Charities, Mrs Clara Fowler, made a will in which she bequeathed a third of her estate, (about £3000) to a fund to provide quarterly supplements to the salary of the curate at Holy Trinity Parish Church. She particularly instructed that this was to be in addition to the normal salary and was either to be administered by the Trustees of the Municipal Charities or by another "Ecclesiastical or other public body". She also left the sum of £1000 to provide a pension for a widow, starting with Mrs Newbrook to whom she was making a weekly allowance. At the request of the Trustees the Charity Commissioners prepared a draft Scheme which was published locally in September 1936 and an Order was received from the Charity Commissioners two months later.

In April 1937 the Trustees were asked to backdate the payment to the curate from the date of Mrs Fowler's death but they refused on the grounds that they could only pay from the date of the investment of the funds. In the same month it was recorded that Mrs Newbrook had died and the Trustees agreed to advertise the vacancy. In 1944 the payments to the widow appointed were six shillings and three pence a week and just under twenty pounds was divided between two curates, presumably for the quarter.

At this time there was a further bequest of £2400 from the sister of Mrs Fowler and this was invested in the fund.

When there was only one curate at Holy Trinity he received all the interest on the capital, less some administrative expenses, when there were two the interest was divided between them and when there was no curate the interest was allowed to accumulate until appointments were made. As a result the lucky man appointed in 1961 received over £124 and two years later a former colleague of the writer was paid the interest for the previous three months between the departure of his predecessor and his appointment.

In September 1966 the Clerk wrote to the Rector, Canon A P Rose, MA to suggest that this charity "would be more appropriately administered by the Church authorities" and he later replied that his enquiries suggested that the Clara Fowler Charity should be administered by the Birmingham Diocesan Trustees.

Early in 1967 the Trustees asked the Charity Commissioners to agree to the amalgamation of the Clara Fowler Widows' Charity with the Victoria Jubilee Aid-In-Sickness Fund and the General Charity and they agreed. The Birmingham Diocesan Trustees, with whom there had been extensive correspondence, were to be appointed custodian Trustees of the Clara Fowler Curate's Fund and Holy Trinity Parochial Church Council were to be appointed Managing Trustees. This was agreed by the Commissioners so the fund became a diocesan and parish responsibility.

In September 1967, following the death of the Clara Fowler Pensioner, the vacancy was advertised and one of the two applicants was awarded the pension at a meeting in January 1968. Unfortunately, she died very soon after and so the pension was given to the remaining candidate but it was then discovered that if she received the pension she would lose state benefits so a vacancy was advertised again. There were two applicants but, presumably, the problem was likely to occur again so in January 1969 the Trustees decided to discontinue the pension. It seems that they were slow to implement this decision because there are no further references to the pension until 1975 when the minutes record that a pension of £12 was still being paid. That was the last reference to pensions in the name of Clara Fowler.

The demise or amalgamation of these small charities in the twentieth century illustrates how, as needs and efforts to alleviate them change, charities have to adapt to the new circumstances if they are to survive. The principal difficulties arise when the money available to meet the objects of the charity is insufficient as inflation develops unless investments provide growth in income to match. Fortunately, the association with Sutton Coldfield Municipal Charities and its greater and increasing resources enabled the charities described earlier to survive for longer than they would have done if completely independent. A second problem is caused by social developments which change needs. For example, improvements in medical provision at childbirth, the introduction of the National Health Service (see also Chapter 8) and the almost complete disappearance of apprenticeships. Such difficulties are exacerbated when the terms of the charity are very precisely defined and where sums of money are prescribed. Fortunately, the Municipal Charities were able to amalgamate with the smaller charities so that their objectives could continue to be met.

Chapter 3

THE TRUSTEES

THE ULTIMATE responsibility for the conduct of several charities in Sutton Coldfield was originally vested in the Warden and Society, the Corporation, but with the establishment of the Municipal Charities when Sutton Coldfield became a Municipal Borough a Board of Trustees was appointed to administer them. For most of the time since 1885 the Board has comprised nominees of the Town Council and co-optative members in varying proportions and numbers as new Schemes were approved by the Charity Commissioners. In the early days the influence of the Council was significant and there were periods when this was accentuated by co-opting Councillors, giving them a majority. From 1974, the proportion of Council nominees has declined and the independence of the co-opted Trustees has correspondingly increased. Because of the considerable responsibilities of the Trustees, who both set policy for the management of the financial and property resources of the Charities and also determine the allocation of funds for grants, they have not only taken advice from professional surveyors, investment managers and accountants but have also sought to co-opt Trustees with expertise in these fields and also in activities which have given them insight into the needs of the community. So, in recent years, the Board has co-opted estate agents, industrialists, solicitors, doctors and teachers as well as people who have had long involvement with a variety of local voluntary organisations. During the same period the Board has been strengthened by the Council nominees who have included people of similar experience and local knowledge.

As the value of the Charities' investments and income and requests for grants has grown, so the need for more commitment of time by the Trustees has increased, especially by the Chairman. The latter, for example, now needs to visit the office once a week in addition to the meetings of the Board and its committees whereas twenty years ago the Chairman would only need to make few additional visits a year. None of the Trustees receives any payment or expenses, except for some light refreshment at meetings and an annual meal together, but all would agree that there is considerable satisfaction in being part of a team which is able to help so many individuals and local organisations.

In 1886 a major change in organisation was imposed upon a reluctant town when a Scheme "for the adjustment of the property, rights, liabilities, etc. of the existing Corporation of Sutton Coldfield" was published and "the Ancient and Royal Town of Sutton Coldfield became after a period of 357 years Corporate existence a modern Municipal Borough, the old title of Warden and Society of the Royal Town of Sutton Coldfield being altered to that of the Mayor, Alderman and Burgesses of the Borough of Sutton Coldfield". (Scheme dated 3rd August, 1885). In paragraph 6 of this Scheme all the property of the Old Corporation which was "within the meaning of Section 4 of the Municipal, Corporations Act 1883, applicable to charity, or applicable to charitable purposes at the passing of that Act" was immediately vested in the "Trustees of Municipal Charities in the Borough of Sutton Coldfield". These were identified as the Rev. William Campbell Riland Bedford, Allen Lepard Crockford, Henry Duncalfe, Thomas Hayward, George Lowe, the Rev. Albert Smith, Samuel Allen Taylor and the Rev. Montagu Webster.

Unfortunately, the minutes of the early meetings are missing so the first records of the new Municipal Charities are for 1894 when five or six of the Trustees were present, although there was one meeting in that year when only three attended. In January, 1895 the Trustees opposed a proposal from the Town Council to increase the number of Trustees to sixteen but two meetings later they resolved that "the Interim Trustees of Sutton Coldfield Municipal Charities wish to increase their number of urgent necessity because four out of eight members are of advanced age and unable to attend the monthly meetings with the regularity which is necessary" (minutes 3.10.1895) and they submitted an application to the Charity Commissioners. Their reply said that changes in the number of Trustees was "to await action by the Council" so in January 1896 the Trustees' meeting was followed with one with the general purposes committee of the Council and at the end of the month the Trustees asked the Council to appoint six additional Trustees, including the vicars of Boldmere and Walmley. With the Rector of Sutton Coldfield and the Vicar of Hill being Trustees this would have brought the total clergy to four out of fourteen, not counting the Rev. Albert Smith who was Headmaster of the Grammar School.

The Council agreed and a joint application was made to the Charity Commissioners who replied that the Town Council, under section 66 of the Local Government Act 1894, was not competent to appoint additional Trustees and suggested that an application be made for a Scheme for a new governing body and also suggested that other charities such as the Lord's Meadow, Jesson's and other charities might be included (see Chapter 2).

The Town Council supported the proposal for a new scheme and the Trustees wanted to widen its scope but the Commissioners refused any changes to the rules on the application of the income. While this was going on two of the Trustees, Allen Crockwood and Henry Duncalfe (Chairman) resigned because of ill-health and the Trustees selected, from four proposals, Henry Horsfall of Penns Hall and Thomas Eddowes, solicitor, to succeed them. The Town Council nominated Ald. William Seal, Ald. Alfred Evans, Alderman John Glover, Ald. Edwin Walters, Councillor Richard Burman and Councillor Edward Brookes and they were accepted by the Trustees. After a misunderstanding about the total number of Trustees the Commissioners wrote again asking the Trustees to apply for a new Scheme and the Trustees agreed to do so whilst asking the Commissioners to approve the appointment of the new Trustees. During the delay there was one meeting in July 1897 when only three Trustees were present.

On 25th January, 1898 the new Scheme was sealed and it included the General Charity, the Lord's Meadow Charity and the Charity of Thomas Jesson. The Trustees comprised eight representative Trustees, appointed by the Council and eight co-optative Trustees who were to be "persons residing or carrying on business in or near Sutton Coldfield and appointed by the Trustees". The normal period of office was to be four years for the representative Trustees and eight for the co-optative Trustees but half of the first representative Trustees were to serve for only half that time. Thus the composition of the governing body which was to last until 1974 was established.

The first Trustees under the new Scheme were:

Representative	*Co-optative*
Rev. John Davis, Vicar of Walmley	Rev. William Riland Bedford, Rector of Sutton Coldfield
William Adcock, Wylde Green, Manufacturer	Thomas Hayward, Esq.
William Seal, Manor Road, Esquire	George Lowe, Esq.

Alfred Evans, High Street, Esquire

Rev. Albert Smith, Headmaster of Sutton Coldfield Grammar School

Edwin Walters, Dow Bank, Auctioneer

Samuel Taylor, Esq.

Richard Burman, Four Oaks, Manufacturer

Rev. Montagu Webster, Vicar of St James, Hill

Edward Brookes, Tudor Hill, Esquire

Henry Horsefall, Esq.

John Glover, Canwell, Esquire

Thomas Eddowes, Esq

There is a lack of consistency in recording professions because, for example, Thomas Eddowes was a solicitor and Henry Horsfall was a manufacturer.

The Rev. Albert Smith was elected Chairman and Ald. Evans Vice Chairman and it was decided that the public (and the press) should be admitted to meetings. This has long since ceased to be the practice although there is now a published Annual Report which summarises the activities of the Charities for the year. Quite frequently however, the Trustees went into committee at their meetings so that the public were then excluded and it is not recorded when all the meetings became private. They decided to form three committees, General Purposes and Estates, Finance and Schools, each with six members and a quorum of three but a year later the Finance Committee was disbanded and each of the others then managed its own finances. The meetings were held at ten o'clock in the morning and two attempts by some Trustees to change the time failed.

In September 1899 the Trustees called a special meeting, at which the public and press were present, to discuss a disagreement with the Charity Commissioners over the application of income. It seems that this may have been provoked by a letter to the Commissioners from one of the Trustees, Alderman Walters, which resulted in a meeting with the Commissioners in London. At the special meeting references to a letter from the Commissioners show that they were concerned that only £96 of the £124 designated for Poor Maidens' Portions (see Chapter 2) was being awarded and that a surplus was being spent on schools and therefore to the relief of ratepayers. The most serious accusation in the letter was that "It therefore appears to the Commissioners that the Trustees are not at the present time observing their trusts and that a new Scheme for the regulation of the Charity has become necessary". They proposed a new Scheme which would allocate two fifths of the net income for Eleemosynary (charitable) purposes and three fifths for Educational purposes. A special sub-committee of Trustees was formed and they wrote a long response to the Commissioners. Clearly, the Trustees were very upset by the accusation that they had been behaving improperly.

Firstly the report suggested that there was a lack of clarity about the ways in which income could be used, especially as the amount increased, and they went right back to the original charter to demonstrate the basis for this belief. They claimed that the Warden and Society appeared "to have arranged for the disposal of the surplus income of the Charity according to their own judgment, and no doubt in the way in which they from time to time conceived to be the most beneficial for the Inhabitants of the Borough at large." (Report of a subcommittee dated 5th October, 1899). They claimed that, following the Elementary Education Act of 1870, they organised the Elementary Schools in Sutton to meet its requirements and considered that the expenditure incurred was in conformity with the "any pious secular use" specified in the original charter and in the spirit of the Scheme of 1825 which made provision for education. Further, they suggested that the Commissioners had approved this application of income because in 1887 "they allowed the debt incurred by the Warden and Society in building the new schools to the extent of upwards of £4,000 to be liquidated out of the capital invested in Consols". (*ibid.*) The new Scheme of 1898 had merely said that after payments for repairs and other property costs and expenditure on administration, any surplus was to be "applied by the Trustees in accordance with the subsisting trusts".

Having delivered this counter attack the committee agreed that there should be a new scheme and also with the proposed distribution of the surplus income between education and charitable purposes since this had been the allocation for some years. They were, however, opposed to any increase in the number of Poor Maidens' Portions as they considered "four quite sufficient for the requirements of the Parish" (*ibid*) as there were usually only four to six applicants but they wanted to increase the allowances to almshouse "inmates" as soon as income allowed and they were willing "to suggest other modes of dealing with a surplus". (*ibid*) Finally, the Trustees asked for an Assistant Commissioner to "be sent down at an early date to confer with them respecting the provisions of a new scheme, and especially with regard to their continuance or non-continuance of the whole or part of the Elementary Education of the Borough." (*ibid*). The significance of the last sentence is that at this time the running of the schools was not in the hands of the Council but was entirely the responsibility of the Charities' Trustees who took decisions on even quite minor matters. (see Chapter 6).

The proposed meeting took place on 29th November at 10.30 am and the Assistant Commissioner declined to allow the public to be admitted as he wanted an informal discussion. It is interesting to note that before his visit and in line with modern practice he asked for a great deal of written information including details of the almshouse residents, a schedule of property and particulars of the recipients of Poor Maidens' Portions. The Trustees had to explain about the premiums paid to apprentices and the duties performed by the surgeon in respect of the payment of £40. The Assistant Commissioner asked to visit the almshouses and agreed with the Trustees that the Mayor and "Representatives of Nonconformists" should be invited.

Unfortunately, there were no minutes of the meeting with the Assistant Commissioner and there are no references to a new Scheme until 1904 but in the meantime there were problems relating to the appointment of Trustees and signs of dissent and other difficulties. Rev. Albert Smith, Headmaster of the Grammar School continued as Chairman until January 1902 although in the previous year it is recorded that Alderman Walters, who had written to the Commissioners, voted against his appointment. In August 1902 Smith resigned and since he wrote from a vicarage in Deddington it appears that he had retired from the Grammar School. At the turn of the century there were frequent changes as Trustees retired but, unfortunately, their departure was often preceded by a period of poor attendance. At the first meeting in 1901 the Clerk recorded that attendances for the previous year included Trustees who had been present for only 1, 2 or 4 meetings and one had not been at all.

One outcome of the extended invitation to the meeting with the Assistant Charity Commissioner may have been a letter from one of those invited, Rev. Frank Collyer who wrote on behalf of members of the Congregational Church. He said that the free churches had a right to be represented on "the Trust of Charities which are municipal and which therefore belong to no one section of the Church". Furthermore, he said, free church members were "a not inconsiderable portion of the Borough" and hoped that two or three of the four vacancies would be offered to free churches, naming five candidates. The Trustees seem to have ignored his request and appointed replacements for retiring clergy Trustees by Church of England priests or laymen. There is no evidence of any discussion of the representation of the free churches from this time up to the present day. No Trustees are identified as representatives and no ministers seem to have been co-opted but some Trustees, proposed for other reasons were certainly members of free church congregations.

In January, 1903 there was the first of several attempts to introduce a Council majority when one of the three names put forward for a co-optative Trustee to replace Rev. Albert Smith was the Mayor, Councillor Vale. During the discussion one proposal was withdrawn and when a vote took place the Mayor was elected by seven votes to five resulting in a Council representation of nine and therefore a majority. This continued for several years until the Charity Commission intervened in 1907.

Very occasionally, the minutes of the Trustees' meetings include a reference to major national events. In June 1900, for example there is a reference to the Boer War when the Trustees extended their condolences to one of their number, Mr Taylor, on the death of his son "who had gone at the call of duty to uphold his country's rights in South Africa". A few months later, at their meeting in February, 1901 the Trustees passed the following resolution:

> "The Trustees of the Municipal Charities of Sutton Coldfield
> desire to place on record their sense of profound sorrow on the
> lamented death of Her Late Majesty Queen Victoria, a gracious
> Sovereign who devoted to her country, revered and beloved by
> her subjects, during a glorious reign of over 63 years, set before
> her people a beautiful example of a noble and consistent life."

Over four years after the criticism of the Trustees' management of the Charities and the meeting with an Assistant Commissioner the Clerk records that there was a letter from the Commissioners which enclosed a draft scheme "determining what proportion of the Corporation Charity should be held for educational purposes and also providing for the future regulation of Lingard's Charity (see Chapter 5) and the eleemosynary portion of the Corporation Charity." This letter also referred to a letter to the Board of Education and one from Arthur Crockford dated November 1903 and asked if these represented the view of the Trustees. At the meeting to consider the letter from the Commissioners it is recorded that the Council had nominated Councillor Vale to replace Alderman Crockford who had been Acting Clerk following the death of T V Holbeche and who had resigned.

There was a special meeting of the Trustees a few weeks later to consider the draft scheme and after the Council had also suggested that the income should be equally divided between education and eleemosynary purposes. The Trustees took the same view and also suggested that the school buildings be transferred to the Council. On behalf of the Trustees, Alderman Burman and Alderman Crockford (acting Clerk) "interviewed the Charity Commissioners" who then issued a draft scheme. There were still disagreements about the allocation of the income with the Trustees wanting to take money for clothing grants from the eleemosynary portion of the income and the Commissioners arguing that it should be taken before the income was divided in half. At this stage the new Clerk, R A Reay Nadin, warned the Trustees that they had been in breach of Orders in Chancery of 1825 and 1828 and they ended the dispute by agreeing with the Commissioners but there were more problems ahead.

In January, 1906 Alderman Glover began a very long term of office as Chairman which continued almost until his death in 1928. At the same meeting the Trustees elected Dr. A H Evans to be Vice Chairman and he continued in this role until 1928 when he succeeded Ald. Glover as Chairman. He was then Chairman from 1928 until 1932 although he continued as a Trustee until 1936, but he attended no meetings in 1934 or 1935. A month later, there was a vote to determine which of two candidates should be co-opted as a result of which Rev. W C Riland Bedford who was one of the original Trustees listed in 1885 was deposed. Not only had they removed the eminent figure of the Rector but, in his place, the Trustees co-opted Councillor Sadler, the Mayor, by a vote of 6 to 5. Thus they again gave the Council a majority of Trustees and did so in the absence of 5 Trustees. At the next meeting, in May they were told that the Charity Commissioners had written a letter setting out their objections which were that, despite an earlier agreement, they had co-opted a member of the Council and that they had done so with only 11 Trustees present. They further said that they considered it "desirable that a further special meeting be held for the purpose of reconsidering the appointment and that all Trustees should if possible attend".

When they met three weeks later one of the Trustees, Mr Ellison who had held office for four years, moved that the appointment of the Mayor be rescinded but the Chairman ruled him out of order and read the minutes of a meeting of the interim Trustees relating to the 1898 scheme. The relevance of these is not clear but it may have been that they refer to the appointment of the Mayor at the time, Alderman Crockford, to replace a co-opted Trustee. A co-optative Trustee, Mr C H Brampton, seconded by Mr Rathbone then moved that "the objections raised to the appointment of Mr Sadler ... are justified and therefore they decline to reaffirm his appointment". At this stage Ald. Seal, Ald. Emery and Coun. Vale left the room and then the motion was put. The

Chairman, Ald. Glover, abstained and the seven co-optative Trustees voted for it so it was carried by a majority of seven.

This was by no means the end of the attempt by the Council nominees to ensure that they had a majority because, later in the same year, when Councillor Bampton retired as a co-optative Trustee on being elected to the Council, the Trustees elected Councillor Randle to be co-opted and also an ex-Councillor. The attendance sheet for 1906 shows 9 Council representatives and 7 others so it is not surprising that the Charity Commissioners intervened again. They noted that one of the provisionally appointed Trustees was a Councillor but said they would approve his appointment unless there was opposition. At the same time they proposed another new scheme to change the composition of the Trustees to 10 appointed by the Council, 3 appointed by the Board of Guardians (one of these to be a woman), 2 appointed by the Governors of the Grammar School and a woman appointed by the Dispensary. One can imagine the consternation with which these proposed major changes were received, not least because the Trustees did not get round to co-opting a woman until 1946! The records simply show that the proposal "was received".

Two months later the Commissioners, despite saying that they would not do so if there were objections, approved the two controversial co-options but also sent copies of letters of protest which they had received and which revealed serious divisions about the control of the Charities. One of the correspondents, Arthur Crockford, wrote that the co-option of Councillors "was distinctly contrary to the spirit of the Scheme" and another, Charles Bamford, wrote that he had resigned his Trusteeship when he became a Councillor "in loyalty to the spirit of the Scheme". His letter also alleged that "a large number of the Burgesses, headed by the Town Council, are determined, if possible, that the whole of the Municipal Trustees should also be members of the Council" and claimed that "the question of the administration of the Charities is made a prominent and burning question at every Municipal Election". This is supported by another of the letters, this time from the Boldmere Burgesses Association, which objected to the co-option of Randle because it was not in accordance with the Scheme of 1905 and was "in direct opposition to the wishes of the inhabitants as expressed at the public meeting in the Town Hall … on September 29th 1904". The approval letter from the Commissioners also said that "although no binding agreement was entered into to the effect that co-optative Trustees should not be members of the Town Council, yet the Commissioners never intended that the body of Trustees should become, as it is now becoming, merely representative of the Town Council" and they went on to suggest that "the management of the Charity should be placed on a more popular basis" and again asked Trustees to apply for a new Scheme. Nevertheless, after all this the Trustees decided not to take any action.

Unfortunately, because the minutes of their meetings only note the appointment of new Trustees and some resignations and the only lists are attendance reports it is not possible to be certain how many Trustees there were at any given time. For example, the report for 1908 shows seven Council representatives who attended regularly but also lists ten others whose attendance suggests that they served only part of the year. However, in 1911 there is a list of Trustees which includes nine Aldermen and Councillors and one other who may have been a Councillor (the Clerk recorded Councillors who were co-opted as "Mr"). Where the composition of the committees, which took most of the decisions about management and disposal of income, are noted there was almost always a majority of Council representatives and never a majority of others.

During the next decade the controversy seems to have died down and, apart from references to resignations and co-options and nominations there is no record of further discussion about membership or any further action by the Charity Commissioners. Considering the major impact which the First World War made upon life in Britain there are surprisingly few references to it at the meetings of Trustees. One of them, Councillor Colonel Green, was absent on military service from at least 1915 until 1919 and either there were few meetings in 1918 or they were not minuted, perhaps because of lack of business. There are some references to the difficulty of obtaining blankets because so many were required by the armed services and the grants committee's lists of applicants for Poor Maidens' Portions show that they were often engaged to servicemen. There were also occasional instances of apprenticeships being extended because the boys were on active service. Throughout the twenties the Council maintained its majority of Trustees, often by nine to seven and continued to retain control of the committees. The most striking example of the imbalance was 1929 when there were ten Aldermen and Councillors to six others although one of these, Sir Alfred Evans was Chairman.

In 1919 the Trustees co-opted Father Lillis who seems to have been the first Roman Catholic priest to serve as a Trustee but there was no consideration of clergy or other representatives of the free churches. Unfortunately Father Willis died almost exactly three years later and his successor in January, 1923 was a layman, Mr Edward Rawlins. When he resigned exactly two years later Rev. Dr. Bird was co-opted to fill the vacancy. He resigned in November, 1932 and the Trustees elected Father Francis deCapitain who was priest at Holy Trinity Roman Catholic Church, to take his place.

In 1926, Dr. A H Evans, the Vice-Chairman was knighted and became Sir Alfred, the first Trustee to be so honoured. He had originally been nominated in 1896, when he was an Alderman, but resigned in 1901 and then served as a co-opted Trustee becoming Chairman in 1929 when Alderman Glover was ill. Later that year Alderman Glover died after being a Trustee for thirty three years of which twenty five were as Chairman. Sir Alfred continued as the first co-optative Chairman until the end of 1932 when he was replaced by Alderman Cartwright. He was co-opted again in May 1934 but attended no meetings in that year or in the next one. At a special meeting in July 1936 the Clerk reported that Sir Alfred had been absent for two consecutive years and drew attention to the Scheme of 1898 which required that this period of absence resulted in his ceasing to be a Trustee. Characteristically, the Trustees put off consideration of this matter until the next meeting and if they took any action then it is not recorded.

Another very long-serving Trustee was Alderman William J. Seal who was first nominated in November 1896 and served continuously until January 1936 when he presumably resigned since the Trustees recorded their thanks for his long service, the last year of which had been as Chairman. Sadly, he died a year later.

In contrast to their elaborate statement of regret at the death of Queen Victoria in 1901 (see above), the Trustees simply record that, at their meeting in January, 1936 at which only nine were present, they "stood in silence to mark the death of King George V". They still had a majority of 9 Council members altogether and had a majority on each of the committees. Five of the Council representatives were on all three committees and there were no non-council Trustees on the Secondary Education Fund Committee which had seven members. The attendance record for 1940 shows eight Trustees who were clearly Council nominees but one cannot be sure that the remainder are not members of the Council. One of them was certainly a County Councillor. The Charities Committee which looked after the disposal of income for eleemosynary purposes had a majority of seven Councillors to six others and on the Secondary Education fund the majority was eight to three but the General Purposes and Estate Committee had six of each category of Trustee. The rather poor attendance of some Trustees e.g. four out of nineteen and three out of ten must also have affected the significance of the lack of balance on the committees. In November 1941 Major A H S Waters was proposed as a Trustee and subsequently co-opted but only after an amendment to elect the first woman Trustees had been defeated. Two months later her name was again put forward and rejected but the seed had been sown.

In 1941 the Trustees found that their expenditure on coal and blankets for distribution to people in need and to almshouse residents was double the amount (£60) set out in the Scheme of 1905 so they asked the Commissioners to increase this amount to £250. In reply the Commissioners suggested a new Scheme and made three proposals:

> The Trustees would pay for the coal and lighting for the almshouses.
>
> The amount available for benefits for the poor to be raised to £100 and this would be in addition to the expenditure on the almshouse residents.
>
> The provision of twenty five shillings a week for a Matron for the almshouses would be changed to "such other amount agreed by the Trustees and approved by the Commissioners".

The response of the Trustees is not recorded but, at the request of nine of them, a new Scheme which included these changes was sealed on 2nd June, 1942.

In November 1944 two candidates for co-option were put forward: Canon E W Brown, who was Vicar of Boldmere, and Miss Doris Burchell who was Headmistress of Sutton Coldfield High School for Girls. Canon Brown was elected by eight votes to four and was duly co-opted. Just over a year later the Council nominated Councillor Mrs Garrard and Councillor Mrs Simpson so for the first time there were women Trustees. For some reason which is not given, Councillor Mrs Simpson was not summoned to any more meetings. By 1944 the committee lists and attendance sheets suggest that the co-option of Councillors had ceased and there were eight Council nominees and eight co-optative Trustees but the occasional practice of describing Councillors or Aldermen as plain Mr may have hidden the true situation from time to time. However, the fairly sparse information in the minutes also suggests that some manoeuvring was taking place because not only was Councillor Mrs Simpson not called to meetings but the attendance list for 1945 shows that Alderman Oldbury had attended all eighteen meetings but was not listed as a Trustee for

1946. From this one might assume that he had ceased to be one but there are no references to his resignation or re-nomination and yet, when the attendance sheet for that year was presented in January 1947, he appears as Mr Oldbury. Had he and Mrs Simpson both been Trustees there would have been a total of seventeen. Some further light is thrown upon this situation by developments during 1946. In January, the General Purposes and Estates Committee made two recommendations:

> "1. That the Co-optative Trustees referred to in Clause 9 of the Scheme dated 25th January 1898, shall not be members of Sutton Coldfield Borough Council and
> 2. That application be made to the Charity Commissioners to amend the Scheme of 25th January, 1898 accordingly."

No further action was taken either by resolution of the full Board or by application to the Commissioners but, in subsequent years the correct balance was maintained and there were no further attempts to create a majority of Council nominated Trustees.

In May, the Charity Commissioners ruled that Mr J A Oldbury would remain a representative Trustee until 27th October and the Borough Council notified the Clerk that Mrs Garrard would remain a representative Trustee, making eight in all. So it seems that Councillor Mrs Simpson was nominated as a ninth representative and it may be that the omission of his title as Alderman was to disguise Mr Oldbury's situation. The last reference to him was in May 1947 when his death was reported to the Trustees. At the same meeting another woman, Councillor Mrs Bryant, attended for the first time but six months later she resigned and was replaced by Councillor F W Terry. At this time changes of Trustees were frequent and in 1947 resignations and new appointments were reported at every meeting.

In some years a better balance was being achieved on committees than used to be the case. In 1946, for example Council nominees had a majority on the General Purposes and Estates Committee, the Secondary Education Fund Committee had equal numbers of Council and co-opted Trustees and the latter had a majority on the Charities Committee but the following year the Council nominees had a majority on the General Purposes (6:3) whilst the co-optative Trustees had a majority on the other two. After that the Council majority continued in most years but, curiously, positions were reversed in

1954 when the Council only had a majority on the Secondary Education Fund Committee. In the absence of a regular pattern it seems that less importance had been given to control of the committees, whose decisions could be accepted or rejected by the full Board, but it is impossible to tell whether this was by design or default.

In 1955 the matter came to a head when the Clerk, R Walsh, wrote a report in which he referred to the attention of the General Purposes Committee having been drawn to "the uneven representation on the committees" and quoted that committee as having nine members and the Charities Committee as having fifteen. The General Purposes Committee and the Clerk also recommended that the Charities Committee and the Secondary Education Committee should be amalgamated since the latter had little business except in September each year. The Clerk then revealed that the reason for the very large Charities Committee was "to avoid members of the General Purposes Committee who are also members of the Secondary Education Fund Committee from leaving until the business of the Charities Committee had been conducted". He set out in detail how the two committees might be constituted to have nine members of the General Purposes Committee and ten on the Education and Charities Committee with at least two members changing committee each year. After consideration of these recommendations the Board agreed that the composition of the committees would be:

> General Purposes and Estates Committee: 3 Council and 5 other Trustees together with the Chairman of the Board and the Chairman of the other committee.
>
> Charities and Education Committee: 6 Council and 2 other Trustees together with the Chairman of the Board and of the other committee.
>
> The Board also agreed to another significant change. Hitherto Board and committee meetings had been held on the same day, usually in the morning. Now the Clerk asked if there could be two weeks between the committee meetings and the Board meetings to allow him to prepare committee minutes for the Board and they agreed.

Frequent changes of Trustee continued and some were able to attend only half of the meetings so the number present at Board meetings varied from only five in January 1956, when they were inquorate, to fifteen in the following year but was usually ten to twelve. Amongst the new Trustees, some are interesting because of later developments. John Joseph Slater, a local estate agent, was co-opted in September 1955 and continued as a Trustee until his death in 1971. His son, also John Slater and an estate agent, was co-opted in 1978 and attended his first meeting in April. He continued as a Trustee until his retirement in January 2005 after almost twenty seven years. In May, 1953 the Council nominated Councillor AGB Owen, OBE, a former Mayor (1951-2), who became the second Trustee to be knighted in 1971, and who continued to serve until 1973. His son, David Owen, OBE, was co-opted in 1983, attended his first meeting in April and continues to be a Trustee to the present day. Because dates of appointment as Trustees are not always available it is, perhaps somewhat invidious to select anyone on the basis of length of service but the minutes of the Board meeting in April, 1962 include a full list which shows that Alderman Arthur Terry, JP was appointed on 27th January 1937 and was a Trustee until his death, which was reported to the Board in April 1967. His continuous service for thirty years was just short of the thirty two years achieved by Alderman Glover up to 1928. It seems that the longest serving Trustee was Sir Alfred Evans who was nominated in 1896 and continued for almost forty years until he ceased to attend meetings. More recently, Colonel Anthony Fender was also a long serving Trustee having been co-opted in April 1971 and continuing until his death, thirty one years later, in August, 2002.

Councillor Mrs Garrard who had been nominated in 1945 continued to be the only woman on the Board, certainly until 1956 when she is listed on an attendance sheet. There is no further mention of her but in April, 1958 Councillor Mrs K E Smith was welcomed to her first meeting so she may have been appointed to succeed Mrs Garrard. Mrs Smith had been Mayor from 1957 to 1958, with Mrs Ethel Wassell as her consort so was it this, in July 1958, that influenced the Trustees to appoint "Mrs Ethel May Wassell, married woman", as the minutes describe her, to be the first woman to be co-opted?

A new Scheme from the Charity Commission was sealed on 27th November, 1968, largely to allow the demolition of some almshouses and for the building of new ones. It set out almost the same constitution for the Board of Trustees except for changes in the period of office. Nominated or Representative Trustees were to serve for four years and Co-optative Trustees for five. However, since the Scheme also permitted the re-appointment of "any competent Trustee the period of office was not really limiting unless either the Council or the Trustees wished to remove a member of the Board. Despite the problems some years before with the co-option of Council members no changes were made in this respect and the only condition set out was that "the Co-optative Trustees shall be persons residing or carrying on business in or near Sutton Coldfield". One further change was that the Trustees were required to establish an Extraordinary Repair Fund for "the extraordinary repair, improvement or rebuilding of the almshouses and other property belonging to the General Charity" by paying £250 and 15% of the gross yearly income from the property into the fund which was to be invested by the Official Custodian.

The Trustees decided to establish two committees: The management Committee to administer the properties and deal with general management and policy, having nine members and the Grants Committee of eleven Trustees to make recommendations about awards and with executive power to make grants up to £50. This structure continued until quite recently except that the limit on grants made by the Grants Committee has been raised from time to time. Two months later the Trustees received a report on the new constitution and future spending policy written by the Clerk and one of the co-optative Trustees, S Dawson Collins. In it they stated that because of growth in income, an increase in welfare services and grants only being made in response to applications there was a surplus of £9,000. In the previous year, the income of the General Charity had been about £19,000 of which £3,000 had been awarded as grants and over £5,000 spent on management and other items. The writers predicted that the requirements of the new Scheme would reduce the payment to the Council for education from £4,000 to £1,000 but the Extraordinary Repair Fund would consume most of the difference. This surplus of about £9,000 would be added to an existing surplus of £42,000 and marked the beginning of a situation which would continue into the 1980s and 1990s when the Trustees, partly in response to pressure from the Commissioners had to consider how to modify grants policies to make use of a considerably increased income. The report suggested more benefits for almshouse residents, communication with doctors and head teachers and invitations to groups to apply for help.

Having considered the report the Trustees decided to continue to provide the almshouses rent free with free lighting and a grant of one ton of coal to each. They proposed to offer grants of coal or other fuel to needy persons, to continue to provide blankets upon application, to make annual clothing grants and to make awards "in certain miscellaneous cases". They agreed to discontinue the pensions paid to almshouse residents from 1st July, 1969. So a pattern for the provision of grants which was to continue until the present was set up, except that the minutes do not record the possibility of making grants to schools and other groups. Such grants now form a major part of the annual distribution of funds.

In September, 1972 with impending changes in local government, the Trustees entered into discussions with the Commissioners about a new Scheme which, it was proposed, would introduce a major change in the balance between the two groups of Trustees. They suggested that the number of Trustees be reduced to twelve of whom four should be nominated by the Council and, since this would be the City of Birmingham Council, they should also be people who were qualified by living or working in Sutton or have special knowledge of the area. The area of benefit should remain unchanged. The minutes of subsequent meetings contain no further references to these changes but a new Scheme was sealed in April 1982, ten years after the discussions, and set out the composition of the new body of Trustees with arrangements for the transition period. There were to be four Nominative Trustees appointed by the City of Birmingham Council and who did not necessarily have to be members of the Council. They were to serve for four years. The remaining eight Co-optative Trustees were to be "persons who through residence, occupation or employment, or otherwise have special knowledge of the area of benefit" (Scheme, 1982) who were appointed at a special meeting of the Trustees and who would serve for five years. From the date of the Scheme Trustees would complete their existing period of office before replacement appointments were made.

There is no record of a Board meeting in April 1974 when re-organisation took place but a list of Trustees from a meeting two months later shows that, with one exception, the eight co-optative Trustees continued in office, the eighth place being taken by a former Councillor, Mrs F M Coombes. The Nominative Trustees were reduced to four of whom three were already Trustees and they were joined by Councillor Fancote, a resident in Sutton Coldfield. A year later she was replaced as a Council nominee by Mrs Coombes and after that it seems that some Honorary Aldermen were being co-opted. In July, 1977, for example, the list of Trustees includes three Councillors (all Conservative) and three Honorary Aldermen so two of the latter must have been co-opted, perhaps because of long service. In June, 1980 the first Labour Councillor, F J Chapman was appointed to replace Councillor Fancote, presumably following the local elections. Since then the Council nominations have tended to reflect the state of the parties on the Council. For many years there were two Conservative and two Labour nominees until the resignation of a Conservative Councillor, after a significant change in the Council, led to the nomination of a Liberal Democrat. Though the number of women Trustees had not increased, one of them, Mrs M Lynall, became the first to be Chairman in January 1983 and she was re-elected the following year. In 1989, Mrs Jean Millington became Vice Chairman and, after two years, she became Chairman in 1991. By this time the Trustees had agreed that, although they would continue to elect their Chairman annually, the normal expectation would be that the Chairman would serve for three years. After a few weeks in this role, Mrs Millington found herself in a unique situation because of the sudden death of the Clerk, Paul Holden Ll.B. Like his predecessors he had been Town Clerk in Sutton Coldfield but after re-organisation he returned to private practice and was employed by the Trustees as Clerk. He had served for thirty one years so when he died the Trustees had to begin the process of finding and appointing a successor for the first time. The second unusual circumstance was that during Mrs Millington's time as Chairman her Deputy became ill and so she eventually served for four years rather then the three planned.

From the first meeting, the Trustees of the Charities had met at the Council House in Sutton Coldfield but after re-organisation in 1974 and because of the very poor state of the unoccupied original almshouses at Walmley they began to consider alternatives. In 1981, work began to convert two of the almshouses into an administration facility comprising a large office and a Boardroom. The first meeting in the new Boardroom took place in April 1983. The other two almshouses were converted into two-bedroom living accommodation for a caretaker, and it later became the home of the Deputy Warden. One of the bedrooms was subsequently provided with access from the Boardroom and converted into an office for the Clerk. In 1994, with a planned increase in staff because of the growth of the Charities, the Deputy Warden was moved to a bungalow on the campus and her dwelling was converted into further offices

By the end of the century, the increase in the capital invested in land, buildings and shares and therefore the income of the Charities had increased enormously, as had the money available for distribution. The commensurate increase in administrative tasks, especially dealing with applications for grants, was met partly by a small increase in the number of staff but there was also an increase in the workload of the Trustees, especially the Chairman who needed to spend time at the offices at least once a week. For several years it had become clear that there was a need for a new Scheme to meet the needs of the Charities and the requirements of new legislation. After lengthy negotiations, the Commissioners agreed and a new Scheme was sealed on 19th June 2001. It stated that there should be a minimum of twelve and a maximum of sixteen Trustees but, unlike the pre-1982 Schemes which required sixteen equally divided between the two types of Trustee, this one made no change to the Council representation. It required that there be 4 nominated Trustees to serve four years and a minimum of eight and a maximum of 12 co-opted Trustees to serve five years, all to be appointed as in the previous Scheme. The new Scheme, for the first time, also formalised the election and office of Vice Chairman and made minor changes to the minimum frequency of meetings. The quorum was again set at five and, for the first time, the Scheme specifically mentioned a committee of at least two Trustees to deal with grant applications between full meetings, provided that decisions were reported at the next such meeting.

From control by members of the Council, often achieved in breach of the requirements of the Charity Commissioners' Scheme, the Board developed a majority of co-opted members and the direct influence of the Council has declined. In recent years, as vacancies occurred, the Trustees have tried to co-opt people with a range of expertise and local knowledge so that they were not entirely dependent upon their advisers. So, for example, they have included successful businessmen, an estate agent, an architect, accountants, doctors, teachers and others with knowledge of groups providing local services. The increase in the number of Trustees not only allows for a wider range of expertise but also of age and thereby helps with acquisition of experience of Trusteeship and the progression towards chairmanship.

Chapter 4

THE PROFESSIONAL ADVISERS

RESPONSIBILITY FOR the conduct of the affairs of the Municipal Charities has always been in the hands of the Trustees but they have been able to take advice from a number of professionals. When the Corporation was established by the Scheme of 1886 all the property of the Warden and Society was vested in the "Trustees of Municipal Charities in the Borough of Sutton Coldfield" so they had a considerable portfolio to manage and one which would require some expertise in legal matters and property maintenance. As the earliest records are not available, the first point of reference is the Scheme sealed in 1898 which gave the Trustees the power to "make regulations for the management of the Charities, the conduct of their business … the deposit of money at a proper bank, and the appointment as Clerk or Secretary during their pleasure of one of themselves (without salary) or some other fit person."

Until the merger of Sutton Coldfield with the City of Birmingham in April 1974 the duties of Clerk were carried out by the Town Clerk and his staff and they also kept the accounts. In 1967, when the Assistant to the Town Clerk retired, he was asked to continue to keep the accounts and was employed for this purpose by the Trustees. Since then they have continued to employ their own accountant.

The first reference to a surveyor was in April 1898 but, when he died in 1934, the minutes mention over forty years' service so he was almost certainly the first one to serve the Charities. Over the years the properties of the Charities have become considerably fewer in number but the value has increased due to improvement in property values and the development potential of much of the land in Sutton Coldfield so the nature of the Surveyor's work has changed. It has also increased as legislation has added to the regulations with which property owners must comply. In the early years, the Trustees approved or initiated repairs and alterations to properties at their annual inspection but in recent times almost all the initiative has been with the Surveyors who have brought proposals to the Trustees, except for a few major projects where the Trustees have suggested developments and asked the Surveyors to investigate.

THE CLERK

The Clerk's role has been to assume responsibility for the administration of the Charities within the Schemes of the Charity Commissioners and the policy decisions made by the Trustees. He has looked after the records of meetings, the correspondence, the management of the almshouses and liaison with the advisers and with the Charity Commissioners. For most of the existence of the Borough of Sutton Coldfield the Clerk was also the Town Clerk and his assistant and his staff did much of the day to day work. In the early years he also had responsibility for keeping accounts and paying bills. Each year the Trustees reimbursed the Town Council for the time which the Clerk and his staff devoted to work for the Charities and the Board and Committees met in the Town Hall.

In 1898 the minutes record that Holbeche and Addenbrooke were appointed as Clerks at a salary of £80 a year, with additional payments for any legal work they did on behalf of the Charities, and they were re-appointed annually. In February 1902, Thomas Vincent Holbeche, who was also Town Clerk, on a part-time basis, was appointed Clerk until his death in early 1904. His death was reported to the Trustees at a special meeting on 17th February and a committee was set up to consider the appointment of a Clerk. They reported in March and the Board resolved that "the gentleman appointed as Town Clerk be appointed Clerk to the Trustees". Two months later documents were being signed by an Acting Clerk whose name was Ellison but in October the Trustees agreed to pay A L Crockford 60 guineas for his services as Acting Clerk. Alderman Crockford, who had been Chairman resigned his Trusteeship, possibly because he had disagreed with the Board over the place of denominational Religious Education in the schools, so he was entitled to be paid.

From October, 1904, the Town Clerk R.A. Reay Nadin became Clerk to the Trustees who met at the Town Hall and paid a fee to the Council for the work done on their behalf by the Town Clerk and his staff. Reay Nadin continued in office until 1937 when, although there is no reference to his retirement or resignation, the minutes of a meeting held in April record that two Trustees,

F Cattell and L. StClair Ford, represented the Charities on a Council committee considering applications for the posts of Town Clerk and Clerk to the Trustees. The appointment of Robert Walsh was reported in July but before he could take up office his predecessor died and in August the Trustees held a special meeting to "mourn the loss of their distinguished and able Clerk who has served them faithfully for so many years and express their profound sympathy with his widow and family at their sad and unexpected bereavement". Thus, after thirty three years, the service of R.A. Reay Nadin came to an end.

At the same meeting, the Trustees appointed Sydney Ashton Stray as Acting Clerk but in November they paid a gratuity of twenty five guineas to a long-serving member of the Town Clerk's staff, A Corbett, for standing in until Robert Walsh took up his duties. In September 1954, the Trustees paid tribute to his work for 39 years as a member of the Town Clerk's staff.

From time to time there were new negotiations with the Town Council on the fees to be paid for the Clerk's services and the variations were sometimes quite significant. In January 1941, for example, the Council asked for £300 per annum and this was agreed but six years later, at the request of the Trustees the fee was reduced to £200.

In January 1957 Robert Walsh became ill and the Trustees appointed J.P. Holden, his assistant to be Assistant Clerk during his "continued indisposition" and on 13th November, 1959 Robert Walsh, OBE, Clerk and Solicitor, retired. The Chairman of the Trustees spoke of the "loyal and indefatigable service for the past twenty two years during which he had endeared himself to this Board by his courteous and characteristic manner".

This time there was to be no *inter regnum* and the Trustees agreed, on 26th November 1959, subject to the approval of the Town Council, to appoint John Paul Holden, Ll.B to be their Clerk and Solicitor and to retain fees in his capacity as Solicitor. The Council required an increase in their fees and the Trustees agreed to the following:

Main Charity	£200
Jesson's Charity	£20
Secondary Education Fund	£100
Victoria Jubilee Aid-In-Sickness Fund	£30

Mr A Corbett, who was still working in the Town Clerk's department retired from that post in April 1967 and from assisting the Clerk from September of the same year but he was employed separately to keep the accounts and continued in that role until 1970.

Paul Holden continued to guide the Charities and anticipated the largest development since the establishment of the Municipal Charities at the end of the last century. He helped the Trustees to prepare for the merger of the Borough with Birmingham in April 1974, especially by obtaining from the Charity Commissioners a new Scheme. In January of that year the Trustees decided that they would employ the Clerk and Solicitor directly and the following terms were agreed to take effect from April 1st:

> "a) the Trustees confirm John Paul Holden Ll.B Solicitor and Clerk as Clerk to the Sutton Coldfield Municipal Charities, at a retaining fee at the rate of £1,000 pa together with all Schedule II fees and expenses properly incurred.
> b) that the appointment and fees be payable for the period until 30th September 1976 and thereafter to be reviewed at intervals of 2 years.
> c) that the Clerk shall be responsible for the safe custody of the deeds, books and valuable records of the Sutton Coldfield Municipal Charities which may be kept at a place convenient to the Clerk provided that the Trustees and the duly appointed agents shall have access to them at all reasonable times."

Paul Holden worked from home until the new offices at Walmley were built and he became a consultant with Blackhams (Solicitors) where he conducted the legal work. During this period the income of the Charities grew considerably and with it the volume of work and the need for expert guidance. In particular there were some major property transactions and an enormous increase in the number and size of grants. As a representative of the Charities remarked after Paul Holden's sudden death on February 17th, 1991 "the guiding hand of this Trust, which brought it from small beginnings to a multi-million charity to be used for the good of all those who live within the boundaries of Sutton Coldfield was indeed a remarkable achievement of this kind and courteous man. He was a man of business and he was able to discuss and handle the many bureaucratic questions from government departments and other official bodies."

When Paul Holden died the Trustees found themselves in a situation which none of them had experienced before and they were fortunate that one of them, Colonel Anthony Fender, who was a very long serving Trustee was able to take over as acting Clerk. Under his guidance an appointment procedure was agreed, the post advertised and, after interviews, Donald Field was selected. His appointment from July 15th, 1991 marked another change because he had no legal training so, for the first time, the roles of Clerk and Solicitor were separated. For the next ten years the growth in activity of the Charities continued and there were more changes resulting from an investigation into the needs of the population of Sutton Coldfield, sponsored by the Charities, and also from changes in the law affecting the management of charities. Meanwhile, Blackhams continued as solicitors and were later joined by Wragg and Co.

In 1999, after an intensive selection procedure the Trustees appointed another former headmaster, Andrew MacFarlane, BEd (Hons) to be their Clerk and he took up office on December 1st working with Donald Field until he retired on January 31st 2000.

CLERKS TO THE TRUSTEES

Dates	Name	Notes
?	Holbeche and Addenbrooke	
1902- 1904	Thomas Vincent Holbeche	Town Clerk
1904 -1937	R A Reay Nadin	Town Clerk
1937-1959	Robert Walsh	Town Clerk
1959-1974	John Paul Holden Ll.B	Town Clerk
1974-1991	John Paul Holden Ll.B	First Clerk directly appointed
1991 (Feb-July)	Col. Anthony Fender TD DL	Trustee and Acting Clerk
1991-2000	Donald J E Field, BSc, MEd, LTCL.	
2000-2008	Andrew M MacFarlane BEd (Hons)	
2008-	Ernest Murray FCIBS	

THE SURVEYORS

The first Surveyor to the Charities was William Fowler who served them for over forty years until his death in 1934. As his appointment was renewed each year it is clear that the Trustees were happy with his work for them and his own commitment to the Charities was evident in 1932 when, as the head lessee of the Tudor Hill Estate he surrendered the lease to the Charities in return for an annuity of £115. 11. 5 for life. This was a very useful gift for them as he died two years later, at which time the income from the estate was £227 a year. His widow, Clara Fowler was also very generous to the Charities, leaving a bequest in her name which provided a pension and additional payments to curates at the Parish Church (see Chapter 2).

The Trustees appointed L.C. Secker of the same firm, Fowler Bewlay, to be their Surveyor and he continued in this role until September 1944 when the minutes record that he was "absent following surgery". Two months later they appointed G.E. Tomlinson, also of Fowler Bewlay, but with different salary arrangements. He was to be paid an annual salary of £200 instead of £100 plus commission and this was the first reference to the payment of commission. Eight years later Tomlinson retired from Fowler Bewlay but the Trustees decided to continue to employ him and he worked from an office in Mill Street where he had an assistant. With the retirement of Tomlinson and his assistant, J.E. Woodward in February 1963 this connection ceased and a new era began.

Soon after, Mr J.H.C. Chesshire of Chesshire Gibson met with Trustees and his firm became the Surveyors to the Charities from 31st March 1963. Since then the firm has undergone several metamorphoses but its successors, DTZ Debenham Tie Leung continue to look after the properties of the Charities and to advise the Trustees on future developments.

THE ACCOUNTANT

Until 1967 the Town Clerk and his colleagues were responsible for dealing with receipts and payments and for keeping accounts but when Mr Arthur Corbett retired from his work in the department he was appointed by the Trustees to continue as their accountant for one year. After that he was re-appointed and continued until 1970 when J.S. Madge took over in September. He retired in 1974 and was replaced by Gordon Hodder who continued until 1977 when R. Dixon was appointed. Seven years later he was followed by Stanley A. (Tony) Ritchie who continued in office until his retirement at the end of 1996. Until this time the accountants, who were employed part-time, worked from home and visited the Charities' office as required but as the number of transactions increased it was becoming clear that closer contact with the other officers was desirable and so, when additional office accommodation became available, it was decided that the new accountant should work from Lingard House. Mr Tim Whiteway was appointed in December 1996.

OTHER ADVISERS

The growth in the value of the capital managed by the Trustees and changes in Charity law which gave greater freedom of investment increased the need for professional advice. Accounts continued to be audited according to the rigorous requirements of the Charity Commissioners and investments which used to be managed by stockbrokers acting under the direct instructions of the Trustees are now controlled within agreed guidelines by professional fund managers. Similarly, the insurance of the properties, the employees and the Trustees are arranged with advice from professional brokers.

During the almost 120 years since the Municipal Charities were set up, the magnitude of the capital base, the income and the funds for distribution have increased enormously so the need for professional guidance and the responsibility of the Trustees have also grown considerably.

Chapter 5

THE ALMSHOUSES

THE FIRST almshouses in Sutton Coldfield were in Mill Street and had been provided under the provisions of the charter of 1528 (Jones, Douglas V., Sutton Corporation, 1973) but in 1737, by order of the Warden and Society, these were demolished and a workhouse was built on the site. When this was redundant because Sutton became part of the Aston Union as a result of the Poor Law Act of 1835, it was altered and became a residence for the master of the school. It was converted into municipal offices, probably in about 1854, and then replaced by a new Town Hall in 1859. After the problems and disputes arising from the management of some of their resources by the Warden and Society, the Master in Chancery set out future requirements in a report dated 14th May, 1825. These included the following:

> "That ten almshouses should be built for the reception of the reduced and meritorious inhabitants, the building of houses being a specific use in the charter, for which there should be allowed the sum of 608*l.*"
>
> (Report of the Charity Commissioners, 19th July 1834)

The report was confirmed by the Court of Chancery and an order dated 3rd August 1825 was made. This allowed the Warden and Society to contract for the almshouses and two small houses to be built and also to appoint:

> "a skilful and proper surveyor, to be appointed by them for that purpose, to cause to be felled such timber in Sutton Park as would be wanted for the erection of the said schools, almshouses and houses"
>
> (op cit)

Later in their report the Commissioners confirm that the buildings erected following this order included:

> "the ten almshouses for poor inhabitants; these contain two rooms each on the ground floor with a cellar below; they are inhabited by ten poor persons or old men and their wives who are elected by the corporation as vacancies occur, but receive no emolument"

The cost of the almshouses in Mill Street was £608 and the two houses for the "sergeant at mace or park keepers, erected in the park" cost £258.

Mill Street The large building on the right was the Town Hall. Next to it are the original almshouses known as the Town Almshouses.

For the first ten years, the only references to almshouses in the minutes of the Municipal charities are concerned with the provision of coal, and payments to the "almshouse inmates" but in December 1896 we find that the almshouses in the town were not the only ones because there is a report of vacancies in almshouses at Hill and Walmley. A year later there is report about fencing at Mere Pool Almshouses but as these are never referred to again it is most likely that these were the ones at Hill (Mere Green). The first time almshouses at Boldmere were mentioned was in June 1900 but many years later, in September 1961, when the Trustees were considering the disposal of old almshouses, the ones at Boldmere and Hill (Mere Green) were described as being one hundred years old. The ones at Walmley, which still survive as offices, bear the date 1863 so they were probably all built at about the same time.

In February, 1897, the Trustees received a letter informing them that

> "Miss Frances Lingard late of Bulls Lane who died on the 15th ult. had bequeathed to the Trustees of Municipal Charities £2700 in trust that within a year of her death" land be made available for building, almshouses erected with the remainder invested for their maintenance, insurance and for payment to residents."

Unfortunately, the good news was tempered by the next sentence which stated that

> "The Executors ... fear that she has bequeathed Charitable legacies to a greater amount than her personal estate which can be applied for Charitable purposes will admit of, and if this is so, the various legacies will have to abate proportionally".

However, by the end of the year, the Trustees heard that the bequest would be paid in full and they instructed an architect to prepare plans which were put out to tender a month later. In March, 1898 Isaac Langley was appointed as builder but the signing of the contract was delayed because there was a problem with the tenant of the land. After the Clerk began an action in the County Court the matter was settled when the Trustees made a payment of £10 for improvements and the tenant, a Mr Bull, gave immediate possession of the land needed for the almshouses and gave up the remainder of his holding in September. The contract with Isaac Langley was then approved in August and the new almshouses were built at Walmley, near to the existing ones, at a cost of £726

9s 6d. The date of completion is not recorded but the first residents, Richard (74) and Charlotte (60) Bush, and Josiah (81) and Maria (60) Dale were elected in June 1899.

The original four almshouses at Walmley. They have been converted to provide offices and a Board Room for the administration of the Charities.

Boldmere Almshouses.

So, when Midgley wrote his history of the town and it was published in 1904 he confirmed that there were twenty two almshouses and that "£340 was last year contributed to the support of their aged inmates." The almshouses comprised the following:

Town	10
Walmley	4
Hill	4
Boldmere	2
Lingard	2

At this time the almshouse residents received two benefits in addition to free accommodation. Each year they were provided with a delivery of coal, often from a local colliery at Cannock, and a small financial allowance. In 1900 this was increased to 10 shillings (50p) a week for a married couple and 7/6 (about 37p) a week for a single person. Inevitably, because many residents were rather elderly when elected, there were quite frequent vacancies as they became too infirm to live on their own or died. Occasionally residents were removed at the request of the Trustees: in March 1897 a woman was removed to the workhouse because "of her failure to keep the almshouse in a sanitary condition" and her allowance was discontinued. At this time the living conditions were of a low standard. There was no water laid on and there seem to have been communal privies but in January 1898 the Trustees agreed that a water supply should be connected to the Town almshouses which were to have one standpipe.

The residents of the almshouses had to sign an agreement to abide by a set of rules and regulations which included a ban on sharing the accommodation and allowed the Trustees to evict them at one month's notice if they were found to be guilty of any "misconduct or disobedience" or were unable to properly care for themselves. From time to time there are references to the removal of residents to infirmaries, relatives or the workhouse because of age and infirmity. In 1913, for example, a single man was removed to the workhouse and another man of 94 who was "very feeble" was removed to his daughter's with a pension of a few shillings.

The regulations also dealt with the procedures for electing new residents and from the lists of applicants there are some illustrations of the social conditions of the time. In 1910, for example, the list included the following:

"Widow, 65, lives with son who keeps her.

Labourer, 62 at sewage farm and wife, 65 earns £1 a week.

Tea seller, does very little work, 68 and wife 67, going blind.
No other income.

Spinster, 61 unable to work because of paralysis, has two
lodgers and no other income."

Vacancies occurred frequently, perhaps because many of the new residents were quite elderly, and when they were advertised there were usually numerous applicants.

Support and supervision of the residents first became an issue in 1900 when the Trustees decided that "two ladies from each District be requested to periodically visit the almshouses and to report to the Trustees on the condition of the inmates and anything further that they think necessary, and that this committee proceed to obtain ladies to do so". A month later the ladies were identified and included Miss Bedford, Miss Webster and Mrs Glover who were relatives of Trustees. We hear no more about support for the residents until January 1917 when the attention of the Trustees was drawn to Miss Stewart "who was elected to the almshouses on the undertaking that she should look after the aged inmates and was not fulfilling this condition of her election". The Chairman of the Charities Committee apparently gave instructions for the Clerk to take possession of the almshouse but as this is crossed out in the minutes, it may not have been carried out.

In 1922 the Charities Committee of the Trustees approved a new set of regulations for the almshouses. No reasons are given for the revision but the new rules are more specific and formed the basis for those which applied until near the end of the century. They included the following:

"Every person occupying an almshouse must be strictly sober.

Must conduct him or herself morally

Must not use profane, abusive or indecent language

Must not quarrel with any of the other almshouse occupants

Must not, without permission of the Trustees by their Clerk in
writing, be absent more than 48 hours from the almshouse

Must not allow any other person, whether relative or not to
reside or sleep in the almshouse unless permission in writing
is first obtained

> Must offer such assistance as may be within his or her power to
> the other occupants of the adjoining and adjacent alms-
> houses."

They further stated that any breach of these regulations "may disqualify the almshouse occupant from being an almsperson and the allowance may be taken away" but it is not stated how the regulations could be enforced except on complaint from another resident, since there was apparently no resident warden.

By January, 1924 there was some concern about the Town almshouses and the Charities Committee asked the General Purposes and Estates Committee to consider selling them and erecting other suitable buildings. A year later a subcommittee had been formed to "go carefully into the question of the removal of the Town Almshouses and to prepare and submit a scheme for such purposes ... at an early date." A few months later it was reported that negotiations with the Charity Commissioners and "other public bodies" were proceeding and the sub-committee had visited almshouses at Yardley in Birmingham. Soon after, the sub-committee recommended the building of ten new almshouses at Walmley, adjoining the existing ones there, and gave instruction for the preparation of preliminary plans. They also suggested that a good price could be obtained for the Town almshouses and asked for a sale notice to be erected. In the meantime, two vacancies were not filled although there were ten applicants.

In January 1926, advertisements inviting tenders were placed in the Birmingham Post and Walsall Advertiser and a special meeting of the Trustees in March agreed to apply to the Charity Commissioners for permission to build ten almshouses at Walmley for an estimated £4,100 of which £1,000 would be met by a subsidy granted by the Corporation. The Trustees also asked for permission to sell the Town almshouses and the site in Mill Street and accepted a tender for building from Mr Pugh for £3995, subject to approval from the Commissioners. Approval was received and building began on June 29th, 1926. The field on which building was to take place was valued by the surveyor at £765 and transferred from the General Estate to the non-educational Charity and an application was made to the Commissioners to sell stock to produce £2,365 to cover the balance required.

At the first meeting in 1927 it was reported that progress with building was satisfactory and that offers for the Mill Street site were being received. Four months later the Trustees agreed to accept an offer of £1,600 and also heard that the new almshouses were completed. In addition they accepted plans for the layout of gardens at Walmley and for entrance gates at an estimated cost of £278 4s 0d. At the end of July the minutes recorded that the new almshouses would be ready for occupation "at an early date and a day and time for opening will be settled at the meeting" but there is no evidence of an opening ceremony after that. A local removal firm, A T Hastilow, was paid £6 for "removing the inmates effects to the new almshouses", curtains were provided and the Clerk won an appeal for a reduction in the rateable value from £9 15s 0 to £3 and £10 each to £4. There was a problem with smoky chimneys in the new almshouses but alterations solved it.

The other almshouses at Walmley and those at Hill and Boldmere had electricity installed in July 1929 which was quite advanced for the times and a year later they were all painted. Strangely, water was not laid on to the original almshouses at Walmley until the summer of 1934. Changes of residents continued to occur quite often due to death or because they had become too infirm to manage on their own. In the latter case they most often went to live with a close relative but occasionally elsewhere. In 1933, for instance, a person from the Walmley almshouses was "removed to the Public Assistance Institution at Tamworth" and a few months later a male resident was allowed to remain after his wife had been removed to Tamworth Infirmary. At about the same time, a couple from Jordan Road, Four Oaks were admitted because of their poor financial situation. They had no pension, had been letting out rooms and selling furniture to survive.

In 1937, the Surveyor and one of the Trustees were asked to investigate a drainage problem with the "new" Walmley almshouses. Unfortunately, because of the level of the external sewers, the main drainage pipe, which drained to each end of the block, was quite near the surface and blockages continued to occur from time to time in subsequent years. With the need to observe the blackout in the Second World War, the Trustees arranged for Taylors of Erdington, who supplied blankets to the Charities, to fit dark curtains to all the almshouses in September 1940. At this time coal was still being provided and the almshouses had open fires but one of the residents was found to have connected an electric bowl fire to one of the lights. It was removed! The open coal fires were still in use ten years later but, in 1947, Miss Bullows, who was then the visitor to the almshouses (see below) suggested that gas should be installed and grillers provided for cooking and the Trustees agreed to the total cost of £270 11s 0d. At this time the Trustees decided to defer a proposal to install a partition to separate the bedroom from the living room in each of the "new" almshouses at a cost of £20 each and decided that consideration would be given to the installation of bathrooms "at some future date".

In August 1942 it was reported that the grounds in front of the Walmley almshouses were in poor condition and the Clerk was asked to obtain quotations for maintenance. Later in the year, Mr Cooke who had a nursery nearby was appointed to cut the lawns twice a month. What other maintenance went on is not clear but we do know that footpaths were repaired in 1947 and that a Miss Scott was paid £1 10s 0d for digging, planting and maintaining gardens in the same year. At the same time the Surveyor was instructed to inform "Mrs Whittaker, one of the inmates … that the practice of her son's horse and cart using the footways leading to the almshouses must cease". Also at about this time the paths to the almshouses were resurfaced.

In 1951 the Trustees again considered improvements to the facilities in some of the almshouses. They proposed the installation of WCs into all the almshouses except the "new" ones by dividing the pantries into two at a cost of £60 per house but the response of the Charity Commissioners some months later was quite long and critical. They suggested that the work could be done in a way which resulted in less cramped conditions and asked the Trustees to consult their architect before sending revised drawings back to the Commission. They also specified how the work was to be financed using housing grants and the funds of the Charities. In August of 1952 the plans and specifications for bathrooms were presented to the Trustees but they asked the architect "to submit further particulars with a view to economising on the cost of the work" and it was not until March 1953 that plans were accepted.

In their letter about the bathrooms the Commissioners said that the money in the Lingard almshouses account could only be used for them but later admitted that these funds were part of the non-educational charity and in 1953 all the Lingard funds were transferred to the General Account of the Charities. The bathrooms were installed in the Lingard almshouses later that year but those in the almshouses at Hill were not completed until May, 1956 and those at Boldmere were completed in September 1957. At this time the "new" almshouses at Walmley still had no bathrooms and they were not added until the following year but the partitions to divide the bedroom from the living room in each one, which had been deferred ten years previously, were erected.

Meanwhile, the four original almshouses at Walmley were in such poor condition that the Mayor wrote to the Trustees about the state of them and asked for "energetic action" to be taken to restore them. The Clerk was asked to prepare a memorandum of the work required and the state of the finances to be sent to the Commissioners and the Surveyor reported that the work needed would cost £3,500. Apparently, these almshouses were void at the time and a tender for £1,028 was accepted for bathrooms to be created in them. About half the cost of putting bathrooms into almshouses was met by improvement grants from the Council.

A few years later, in July 1961, the Trustees set in motion a major development when they decided that they would no longer fill vacancies at Boldmere and would investigate the sale of the site. The Clerk met the Charity Commissioners in London and they suggested that they would not oppose the sale of the Boldmere and Hill almshouses when they received a detailed application. At Boldmere the two houses were about one hundred years old and the site was zoned for housing. One resident was in hospital and one was aged 90 years. At Hill (Mere Green) the four houses were about the same age and the area was zoned for shopping. In April 1963 the Trustees agreed to sell the almshouses at Hill and some adjacent land to a developer for £18,500 and, a few months later, the Commissioners agreed to a sale, with about £15,000 being spent on a new residential development. The sale was completed in July 1964 and Donald Grove (later a Trustee) was appointed architect to design a scheme for new dwellings at Walmley. It was proposed that there should be a first phase of ten houses and a second one to be decided at the annual inspection when the Trustees visited the properties. Meanwhile some improvements were made with gas cookers being provided in the Boldmere and Walmley almshouses in 1964 and new electrics at Walmley in 1965. As the Council refused to surrender the lease of land at Walmley needed for the new almshouses until July 1967 building was delayed and in September 1966 planning consent was refused. At this time negotiations were proceeding with the County Education Committee for the Boldmere site and the Trustees agreed to their offer of £2,700 which was then approved by the Charity Commissioners and the deal was completed by April 1968.

The planning application for developments at Walmley went to appeal in 1967 and was again refused because of the access width and the elevation to Walmley Road but it was reported in October 1968 that revised plans had been approved. Six months later the Trustees agreed to go ahead with a scheme which would cost £54,666 and which would comprise 13 dwellings, warden's accommodation, and a residents' room. The cost was to be met by the proceeds from the sale of almshouses at Hill (£16,000) and Boldmere (£2,700), accumulated income in the General Charity (£30,000) and either the sale of securities or money awaiting investment (£11,300) but applications for grants were made to the County Council and the Ministry of Housing and Local Government. Tenders were invited from six contractors and Davis and Son who submitted the lowest one at £55,820 were selected. To this had to be added architects and quantity surveyors fees and furnishing and gardening costs amounting in total to £7,350. By January 1970 the Trustees had agreed that the Council would pay an annual grant to the Charities as a housing association for a period of 60 years after the completion of the buildings. There are no records of the progress made with the new almshouses but in January 1971 it was agreed that the Charities should advertise for a Warden and that a short list would be interviewed by the three Chairmen and Councillor Mrs Dunnett. At the same meeting they agreed to provide curtain rails and fittings in the new dwellings, to charge £1 per week for electricity in the almshouses and to continue to supply a ton of coal a year for the old almshouses. At the next quarterly meeting the Trustees were told that the handover of the new buildings was complete, that the 13 new dwellings had been allocated from over fifty applicants. Mrs Allworth had been appointed Warden, estimates for the layout of gardens approved and furnishings for the new Common Room were also approved.

On 26th May, 1971 HRH Princess Anne performed the official opening ceremony. She went first to the Town Hall and after meeting representatives of the town and county she had tea with them. There was then a procession by car comprising HRH Princess Anne and a Lady in Waiting, The Lord Lieutenant and his party, The Mayor (Alderman Mrs E Dunnett), The Town Clerk (who was also Clerk to the Trustees) and the Chairman of the County Council. On arrival at the almshouses, the Chairman of Trustees introduced the Surveyor, the Architect and the contractor to the Princess. A plaque and a signed photograph hanging in the Common Room were unveiled by the Princess and she was presented with a riding crop. She then met the Warden and several residents and visited one of the new flats before leaving. The invited guests adjourned to Penns Hall Hotel for cocktails and, perhaps something more substantial.

At the next meeting the Trustees agreed to buy more chairs, to rent a television set and to advertise for a piano for the residents' lounge. The final

Mere Green shops. Now awaiting demolition and redevelopment.

The school at Roughley. Now a dwelling attached to a farm shop.

School at Mere Green. Formerly used by St Joseph's School and as a Teachers' Centre.

Almshouses built from the bequest of Frances Lingard in 1898. In 2009 major works were carried out to bring them up to modern standards (see colour illustration).

Wylde Green School, Green Lanes, the only one still in use as such.

The present day Horse and Jockey pub.

Duke Street School. Now used for pre-school education.

The Cup pub in 2009.

The Lord's Meadow.

Former landfill site at Manorial Farm.

Sutton Coldfield Baptist Church (formerly Town School).

Emmanuel Court. Offices to rent, purchased 1990.

Almshouses in Walmley Road, opened 1927 and extensively refurbished.

The Lingard Almshouses recently refurbished.

Wardens' Flat (upstairs) and Residents' Lounge (ground floor), opened 1971.

Flats and bungalows, opened in 1971.

Last almshouses, opened in 1995.

cost of the new buildings amounted to over £62,000 and, having completed that project, the Trustees began to plan improvements for the 1927 almshouses on Walmley Road, including the installation of electric storage heaters, roof retiling and the lowering of chimneys, with the aid of improvement grants of 50% from the Council.

One of the improvements introduced at about this time was a system which allowed any resident to call the Warden directly from several pull cords in the dwelling and which also allowed calls in the reverse direction so that the Warden could contact each resident to see how they were. In the 1990's, following some well-publicised accidents in sheltered accommodation elsewhere, it was decided to require the Warden to contact each resident daily to check on their well-being and later a more sophisticated system allowed the contact to be by a detachable telephone handset with a range which allowed the Warden to be anywhere within the grounds or even at the local shops.

In November 1972, when one of the Lingard almshouses was unoccupied, the Management Committee suggested that these be demolished "at the appropriate time". However, the Trustees had second thoughts and, a few months later, approved a scheme to modernise them at a cost of £9,240 with an improvement grant of £2,000. By January 1975 it was reported that the work would be completed by Easter and that two residents from the oldest almshouses would be moved in so that the ones vacated could be demolished like those at Boldmere and Hill. Later that year a planning application was made to convert them into two dwellings with car parking but when the Secretary of State imposed a Building Preservation Order upon them almost a year later the Trustees decided to put them up for sale. Three months after that there was another change of policy when estimates were obtained for "possible improvements" but not long after that decision another application for planning permission to convert them into two dwellings was made. The outcome is not known but a year later the architect, Donald Grove was asked to prepare modernisation plans and in January 1979 he presented proposals to convert these old almshouses for administrative use at a cost of about £30,000, to include an office, a boardroom and some living accommodation.

In October 1979 the Trustees heard that planning permission had been refused quite comprehensively because of "noise, disturbance, inadequate parking, loss of residential accommodation and inappropriate development". Since the almshouses which the Trustees wished to replace were well below current standards and the proposed changes were to provide accommodation for two people together with office space for two part-time staff the objections were difficult to understand and the Trustees decided to seek further consultation with the Planning Committee and, if necessary to appeal to the Department of the Environment. As there is no record of an appeal it seems that the discussions with the planners were successful because two years later the Trustees gave approval for the conversion to begin at an estimated cost of £65,000. Two of the almshouses became an office and a boardroom with kitchen and toilet facilities and the other two were converted to a single dwelling with kitchen, living room, bathroom and two bedrooms, occupied at first by a caretaking couple and later by a Deputy Warden. The first meeting in the new boardroom took place in April 1983.

As the disposable income of the Charities and the number of grants increased an additional secretary was appointed so, in 1988, one of the bedrooms of the Deputy Warden's flat was converted into an office for the Clerk and connected to the boardroom. A few years later, in 1994, as the number of staff increased to deal with the growing administrative work resulting from further growth of the Charities, the whole of the building was taken over and the Deputy Warden moved to one of the single storey dwellings.

Meanwhile, further improvements to the almshouses built in 1927 were carried out. Double glazing was fitted in 1988 and a few years later damp courses were injected and the toilets were further insulated in a successful attempt to deal with longstanding problems with dampness. Because of safety considerations, electric storage heaters were installed and gas supplies were discontinued.

In 1990, another almshouse trust, the Hook Memorial Trust was also facing difficulties because of its inadequate and outdated accommodation so the possibility of amalgamation was discussed and outline agreement reached. The Municipal Charities were to consider further building at Walmley and agreed to perpetuate the name of the Hook Memorial Trust. Later it emerged that the approval of the Charity Commission would not be given because of differences in the areas of benefit. The Municipal Charities being confined to supporting people from within the boundaries of the former Corporation and the Hook Memorial Trust having a larger area of benefit. The Hook Memorial Trust later merged with the much larger Lench's Trust and the site was redeveloped to provide modern dwellings.

The final development at Walmley took place when the old clinic building on Walmley Road reverted to the Trustees who also purchased an adjoining house and garden. Three new almshouses were built on Walmley Road and opened in October 1994, followed by a further five along the end of the site. These were all to a very high specification and were occupied in May 1995. The official Opening Ceremony was performed by Robert R Taylor OBE, K.StJ, JP, Lord Lieutenant of the West Midlands. Since then the Trustees have begun a long running programme of improvements to the other almshouses to produce very comfortable dwellings to a high specification in attractive and secure surroundings.

One of the factors that encourages people to apply for almshouses and which the residents value is the support provided by the wardens. Since the establishment of the Municipal Charities the improvements to the facilities in the almshouses have been matched by developments in the care of the residents. The first copy of the regulations for the almshouses relates to 1899 and they deal mainly with the procedures for advertising vacancies by posting notices on "the Door of the Town Hall and all Churches and Chapels in the Borough for two consecutive Sundays", procedures for appointing residents and the arrangements for vacating the dwellings. As described above, support and supervision of the residents first became an issue in 1900 when the Trustees decided that "two ladies from each District be requested to periodically visit the almshouses and to report to the Trustees on the condition of the inmates and anything further that they think necessary, and that this committee proceed to obtain ladies to do so". In 1917 there is a reference to Miss Stewart "who was elected to the almshouses on the undertaking that she should look after the aged inmates and was not fulfilling this condition of her election".

There is no further information about supervision until 1936 when the minutes of a Board meeting record that there were satisfactory reports on the almshouses from the Hill and Four Oaks Nursing Association but by 1941 a Miss L Vale was being paid £20 a year to report on the "almshouse inmates" and to pay their weekly pensions. In 1944 Miss Ruth Bullows was appointed to visit the almshouses with an honorarium of £30 and she continued to provide reports for the Trustees until she retired in April 1952. Her replacement was Miss E M Grubb, a former Health Visitor who was paid £52 a year, including the use of her car. No reports are recorded and in 1962 her allowance was increased to £75 a year but there is no information about her subsequent retirement.

When the new almshouses were planned the accommodation included a flat for a resident Warden and the post was advertised in 1971. The requirement was for a lady warden at £5 per week with accommodation provided and rates paid. Candidates were interviewed by the three Chairmen of the committees together with Mrs Dunnet and a Mrs Allworth was appointed. Later, a Deputy Warden was appointed and since then there has been full-time emergency cover for the residents who also receive all the services provided by the National Health Service and by Social Services to which they are entitled. The regulations have evolved to meet modern requirements and have been subsumed into a user friendly handbook. From time to time the Trustees considered the possibility of using one of the centralised emergency call agencies but decided to continue with their own warden system for the time being. In recent years new legislation about working conditions and the need to reduce the hours when time on call was counted as working time compelled the Trustees to use a centralised care agency when the wardens are off duty. Considerably improved social conditions have changed the needs which lead to applications for vacant almshouses but today's residents appreciate their sheltered and comfortable living conditions, the benefits of being members of a small community and the security of knowing that in the event of difficulty they can call for assistance from the care agency or the wardens whom they know and trust.

Chapter 6
THE SCHOOLS AND EDUCATION

ONE OF the areas of responsibility transferred from the old Corporation to the Municipal Charities by the Charter of 1886 was the school system, except for Bishop Vesey's School. The origins of the elementary schools were in a series of disputes between residents of Sutton Coldfield and the Warden and Society towards the end of the eighteenth century. There had been complaints that the Warden and Society (the Corporation) had allowed strangers to graze their cattle in the park and had permitted trees to be felled and had used the profits for their own purposes. A group of townspeople petitioned the Lord Chancellor in 1788 leading to an injunction granted in 1792 which restrained the Corporation from felling any more timber and impounded the profits. According to Midgley (1904) the lawsuit "dragged along for nearly forty years and by the end of that time a sum of over £40,000 of Sutton money had accumulated in the Chancellor's hands."

A committee which had been set up by the Corporation to negotiate with the relators (those who had petitioned the Lord Chancellor) prepared a plan to use the accrued money and, after it had been presented to the Corporation and the relators, it was discussed at an assembly held in the Moot Hall in April 1808. It was called "A Scheme for the application of the increased Revenue of the Corporation of Sutton Coldfield" (Redwood) and included a proposal to establish a charity school for "the moral and religious instruction of the Male and Female Children of the Poor Inhabitants of the Parish". It also proposed that a similar school be set up in Hill (Mere Green). The children were to be under seven years of age and money was to be set aside for building and furnishing the schools, for fuel and for the salaries of the Masters or Mistresses.

It was also proposed that a School of Industry be built for 30 girls who would be instructed in sewing, spinning and knitting, together with writing and arithmetic. These activities were to be practical since the girls were to make clothing for themselves and for the girls at other schools, to knit "stockings for the boys" and also to "make up Linnen for the Poor unmarried Women in Child bed" (see Chapter 2).

In 1813, the Rector, John Riland, presented a petition from a committee of residents asking that the money be used to establish elementary schools and this was supported by those who had petitioned the Lord Chancellor (the relators) and also by the Master of the grammar school. Unfortunately, there was no immediate result but in May 1817 agreement was reached and the Corporation accepted a "Scheme for the appropriation of the increased revenues of the Corporation" to be submitted for the approval of the Master of the Court of Chancery (Redwood).

The Corporation Boys and Girls National Town School (Town School) circa 1870 from Lower Parade. This school opened in 1820 but was eventually sold to the Baptist Church and has been extensively refurbished.

The Scheme proposed the establishment of a Charity School for the "moral and religious instruction of 100 male and female children of the poor inhabitants of this Parish" using the monitorial system devised by Andrew Bell and Joseph Lancaster. Under this system pupils were grouped by ability and the top group was taught by a qualified teacher but its members also spent time teaching the other groups. It was claimed that this system not only provided low cost education but also trained working class children for responsible jobs in he future. This eventually became the Corporation Boys and Girls National Town School which opened on 23rd January 1826. The term National School indicates that the school was set up to observe the principles of the National Society for Promoting the Education of the Poor in the Principles of the Established Church Throughout England and Wales established in 1811. This was to become a basis for controversy at the beginning of the next century when major changes in the schools resulted from a new Education Act.

A similar school to serve Hill and Little Sutton was also proposed, together with a preparatory school for 40 children at Walmley. The School of Industry was to be at the Town School and the buildings were to cost £1,200. The Masters of Town and Hill schools were to be paid £40 a year, the Mistress at Walmley would receive £25 and the Mistress of the School of Industry was to be paid £60 a year from which she was to employ an assistant. Children would enter school at the age of six and leave when they were 12. The sum of £2 per boy and £1 11s 6d per girl was allowed for clothing which comprised, for the boys, a blue cloth jacket and trousers, shirt, stockings, woollen cap and shoes. The girls were to wear a blue cotton frock, straw bonnet, shoes and stockings and a cloak and all the clothing was to be made locally. Just as in modern times, the school building programme was over budget and the Court of Chancery was asked to release a total of just over £1,000 for extra work. There was also an extra £300 to enlarge the galleries in Holy Trinity Church to accommodate the children.

Hill School was erected in 1826 and catered for 25 boys and 25 girls. The Master and Mistress, who were Mr and Mrs Daniel Aulton, were paid £60 a year and provided with accommodation. Walmley School, which was originally for 10 boys and 10 girls was built between 1826 and 1827 at Signal Hayes Road, Thimble End when a temporary head teacher, Mrs Thomas Short was replaced by Miss Sarah Adams who was paid £25 a year and also received a free supply of fuel. She had a dwelling next door and the building could accommodate 60 children. It was also used for worship until the parish church was built in 1845 and a bigger school was built next to the church in 1851. At this time the original building was converted into two cottages.

In 1838 another school was built in Green Lanes, Wylde Green and this was for boys from quite a wide area. The school master lived on the premises and

The school at Hill (Mere Green) erected 1826. Formerly a restaurant but now a pub (The Old Speckled Hen).

Walmley school.

was paid £50 a year together with £5 for fuel. A similar school for girls was later built at Boldmere. The Education Act of 1870 aimed to make education for all compulsory and set up School Boards to administer the schools. St Joseph's, the first catholic school was built opposite the church (behind the present day one) and opened in 1878.

An additional building for Town School was erected in 1870, when elementary education became compulsory. Because there had been outbreaks of scarlet fever, diphtheria and other illnesses the school was visited in 1873 by the Rector, Rev. W K Riland Bedford, a surveyor and a sanitary inspector to examine the drains but with little apparent effect since there was an outbreak of scarlet fever in 1876 and the school was closed for three months. All the classes were taught in one room, designed for 84 children but which by 1898 accommodated 203. Until 1889 there were no wash bowls and the drinking water tap was next to the two earth closets so poor hygiene, overcrowding and inadequate ventilation provided the classic conditions for the spread of infection.

After the Municipal Charities assumed responsibility for the schools from 1886 the first records available (May 1894) show that the Trustees were not just concerned with general policy but became involved in the detailed management of them, dealing with matters ranging from the erection of an additional classroom at Boldmere to the provision of stop taps at Hill School and the purchase of basic supplies. In October 1894 the new vicar, Rev. E R Bedford, was deputed to "inspect the school registers and see that Pupil Teachers receive their lessons" and in the following months the Trustees appointed a mistress to Roughley Infants School, refused permission for Boldmere School to be used by the Silver Star Minstrels for a public concert and organised prize giving in the Town Hall for girls and then boys. There is no record of an administrator, other than their Clerk, and there is no evidence that the Masters and Mistresses who were in charge had any involvement in the administration of the schools. Nevertheless, even in those days, it appears that teaching may have involved some stress, although it was not identified in this way, because in March, 1895 the Trustees granted thirteen weeks' absence to Mr Field, the Master of Hill Boys School for a sea voyage to recover from ill health and in November of that year the retirement of Mary Groom, the Mistress of Town Infants School after 23 years due to "failure of health" is recorded.

Although the minutes of the Trustees' meetings refer to the schools by name, the first definitive list of schools does not occur until an inspection in 1902. The report, entitled "Reports of His Majesty's Inspector upon the Various

Elementary Schools in the Borough of Sutton Coldfield for the Year Ending 30th June, 1902" includes a table listing the schools, the number of places available and average attendance as follows:

Name of School	No. of Places	Av. Attendance Year end June 1901	Av. Attendance Year end June 1902
Town Boys	293	241	264
Town Girls	176	183	187
Town Infants	81	97	82
Maney Infants	74	74	72
Boldmere Girls	175	94	105
Boldmere Infants	150	104	120
Green Lanes	143	105	136
Hill Boys	128	120	120
Hill Girls	136	66	79
Hill Infants	74	73	65
Roughley Infants	74	28	31
Walmley Girls	81	47	47
Walmley Infants	77	54	52
Totals	**1,662**	**1,286**	**1,360**

These figures show that the efforts of the Charities to correct a shortage of places in some of the schools (see below) had been successful but that the modern imbalance between the number of school places and the number of pupils existed in those days. So, whilst Town Girls School was oversubscribed and several others were nearly full, Hill Girls, Roughley Infants and Walmley Infants had many spare places. The very brief comments from the Inspector are in sharp contrast with modern inspection reports but illustrate that although the reports are generally good some of the problems have not changed:

> Town Boys – "The marked improvement … shows that sufficiency of staff is required … to produce first-class results."
> Town Infants – "Considering the conditions under which work has to be done, the general efficiency continues to be creditable."

Maney Infants – "… A more vigorous exercise of the Teacher's will is required to enforce and maintain proper discipline and attention … much of the teaching is barren in the lower classes."

Boldmere Infants – "Though the children are not disorderly, they are not so attentive and interested as they should be"

Green Lanes School – "accommodation is insufficient for the average attendance …"

Walmley Infants School – "The cause of the bad smell should be ascertained. The nuisance … is understood to have existed for some years and should be remedied as soon as possible."

The inadequacies of the buildings and the ill-health of pupils seem to have been problems which were reported from the time when the Municipal Charities became responsible and which occasionally caused the Trustees to

Boldmere School.

Boldmere Infants School 1938.

receive critical reports from officers of the Corporation. In June 1896, for example, a letter from the Town Clerk complained of the poor attendance at Boldmere School which was "due in some measure to the management prevailing there". In reply the Mistress explained that poor attendance was due to sickness. Two months later the Health Committee of the Council complained of water in the cellar of the Master's house at Hill Boys School and that a notice to abate the nuisance had not been complied with. When threatened with a summons, the Trustees informed the Town Clerk that "steps were being taken"! However, in January of the next year another letter from the Council was received insisting that something be done about the six inches of water in the cellar, provoking the Trustees to respond that they were "much surprised at the tone of the letter" and were taking action to lay tar outside to take away surface water. Interestingly, the Town Clerk writing for the Council and the Clerk to the Trustees was the same person, Thomas Holbeche. At the same time "sanitary works" at Green Lane School and Maney Infants School were to be carried out because the Inspector of Nuisances had complained to the Trustees about the privies at Green Lanes and Duke Street Schools and required them to be converted to Water Closets.

To be fair to the Trustees they were not free to make improvements to the buildings they had inherited because, in 1896 when the Trustees put forward proposals to do that, the Charity Commissioners raised objections. A letter from them referred to the "undesirability of the Trustees incurring any so considerable expenditure upon these schools while the propriety of the expenditure is still under consideration" but two months later they allowed the Trustees to spend up to £1,500 on Town School "because the matter would seem to be pressing".

There is another reference to the health of pupils in the minutes of a meeting held in June 1898 when the Board considered a request from a Dr. Hobbes for a salary increase. His reasons included the need to visit urgent cases in their own homes and that he had been providing medicines and surgical appliances from his own money. On the grounds that they had inadequate funds his request was refused by the Trustees and he was re-appointed at £40 a year with the promise that the Trustees would make further enquiries. Unfortunately, there is no reference to the matter until two years later when the payment of his salary, but not the amount, is recorded.

In August, 1898, a special committee agreed to send a circular to ratepayers asking for contributions for "additional means required for carrying on the Elementary Schools" and 2,173 were issued. By January of the next year the amount raised was just over £100 but reminders had been sent out so that a month later the amount had risen to £134 and this sum was placed in a suspense account. It was not until April, 1903 that this money was transferred to the general account, probably because of the imminent changes arising from the Balfour Education Act of 1902 which set up Local Education Authorities.

Although plans for a new infants' school were approved by the Trustees at the end of 1898, when the estimated cost was £950 there were delays while the permission of the Charity Commissioners was obtained and the plans were approved by the Education Department. In May, 1901 the Trustees agreed to accept a tender of £1,200 from a Mr J M Smith and in August the Clerk reported that the Charity Commissioners had approved the raising of £2,000 from the sale of investments and the builder was paid £600 on account. He proceeded very quickly because a meeting on 5th December was told that the building was completed and would be occupied after Christmas.

In the same year, the Board of Education gave approval for the enlargement of Town Girls School by 40 extra pupils, Maney Infants by 27 and Hill Infants by 32. The plans for Town Girls School were rejected at first because the rooms were too narrow but, after modification, they were approved and a tender from Isaac Langley for £725 was accepted so that work began on May 3rd 1902.

The Trustees continued to be involved directly in the management of the schools. Each school enlargement created a need for additional furniture and, as head teachers sent in a request, individual Trustees were asked to make the arrangements. So, for example, after the Master at Green Lane Schools asked for more desks in August 1902, Councillor Adcock was deputed to "purchase what is necessary" and 15 double desks were purchased. Similarly, in December of the same year, £50 was allocated for furniture for the new classroom at Town Girls School but a later note shows that £38 5 0 was spent on 30 locker desks. One intriguing purchase was an "unclimbable gate" for Town Boys School and, despite his many other responsibilities, the Chairman was asked to purchase the cleaning materials for all the schools at the beginning of 1902.

One major task was the appointment of teachers and decisions about their pay. In the absence of national pay scales teachers applied for individual increases and most meetings had to deal with such requests. In 1899 a special committee was set up to determine salaries, except for head teachers, but it seems to have rapidly been abandoned since, only a month later, the Trustees were dealing with staff appointments and salaries at their regular meeting. Later an Assistant Teacher was appointed to Town Boys School, a new Head was found for Maney Infants School, the Head of Hill Boys was refused a salary increase but one was granted to an assistant at Town Girls School. A further attempt was made to rationalise salary consideration in May 1902 when the Trustees decided that "in future no applications for increases in salary would be considered except at the April and October meetings."

The Trustees kept a close eye on attendance with regular register inspections and appointed some of their number to be School Visitors of whom all except one were clergymen. They also dealt with school hours and holidays and attended personally to present prizes each year for good attendance. To qualify at Town School, the pupils had to achieve at least 400 attendances, although this was reduced to 380 if they lived more than a mile away. In December, 1899 the Trustees agreed to a suggestion from the staff at the Walmley school that the afternoon session be moved forward to 1pm from 3pm because parents had complained that children reached home after dark, An outstanding case occurred in August 1900 when they agreed to subscribe for a special prize for

May Storer who had attended Town Girls School for eight years without a single absence. She was fortunate to escape the epidemics which affected the schools from time to time, one of the most serious occurring in February, 1903 when Boldmere Infants School was closed for three weeks due to measles. It is also recorded that the schools were closed on 26th and 27th June, 1902, those being "the days of the Coronation Festivities".

Another break from school routine for some boys is noted in June 1898 when 30 from Town School and 15 from each of the other two schools were made available to work at the Royal Show, having been chosen by three Trustees who were clergymen. The event was held in Sutton Park near to the former Four Oaks Hall where King Edward VII had lunch before visiting the Show. Nothing further is known of this activity and what part the boys played but in the following March the record of a meeting shows that the Royal Horticultural Society paid over "the balance of the local fund" (over £35) towards the maintenance of schools so a financial consideration was involved.

In March 1901 the Trustees considered a recommendation from the schools committee that they should contribute £5 towards the cost of a piano for Town Girls School where a concert by pupils and staff had raised £16. For reasons which are not given they referred the request back for further enquiries but the grant was made a month later. It is probably not a coincidence that an almost identical request was received from Boldmere Infants School in the following year. No details are given, but there are several references in the minutes of meetings to payment for swimming lessons given by Sutton Coldfield Swimming Club. They were apparently given only to boys and are first mentioned in June 1898. In the following year the payment was £2 10 0 and the lessons continued at least until 1902 after which they are not referred to again, perhaps because of the major changes which dominated the Trustees' meetings from then on.

The Order in Chancery under which the schools were established also required that clothing was provided for 120 boys and 120 girls and this practice continued after the Municipal Charities became responsible for the schools. In 1898, for example, the clothing, which was selected by one of the Trustees, included pilot suits at fourteen shillings and sixpence, cord trousers at five shillings and fourpence and caps at one shilling and threepence for boys and girls' hats at nine shillings and a farthing each. The clothing was distributed in proportion to the number of children and the average attendance so in that year the allocation was as follows:

Town Boys	58	Town Girls	62
Green Lanes	32	Boldmere Girls	35
Hill Boys	25	Hill Girls	21
Catholic Boys	5	Catholic Girls	5

In the following year there was a similar distribution except that the list included Walmley Girls School where there were nine recipients. Although not included in the clothing list, boots were also provided. In 1900 the Trustees approved the purchase of the following materials for school clothing: 230 yards of flannel, 439 yards of scoured grey calico, 120 yards of Holland, 720 yards of brown calico and 80 yards of white calico. There is also a note that Emma Stonehouse was paid for the cutting out of school clothing. The thirty girls in the School of Industry attached to the Town School made up the clothes and also knitted stockings for the boys (see above). Later that year it was decided that serge would be provided rather than Winsey for the girls.

The last reference to the provision of clothing was in 1903 when the purchases comprised 120 Pilot Cloth Suits (these were made from a felt-like material with jackets like a sailor's pea jacket), 120 cord trousers, 120 Pilot Cloth Caps, 563 yards of Navy Blue Serge, 2 pieces of blue nap, 120 girls' hats and 144 pounds of black wool. Distribution was again based upon attendance and the number of children in the school. Later, grants were made to needy parents to help with the purchase of school clothing (see below and chapter 8)

By this time momentous changes were about to take place and, for the second time there was to be resistance to them. Sutton Coldfield had been one of the last towns to become a Municipal Borough and only did so when forced under the terms of the Municipal Corporation Act, 1882. In 1870 the Elementary Education Act provided for School Boards to be set up to consider the education provided in their districts and, if necessary; to create new schools and to pay fees for the poorest children. Ten years later another Education Act made attendance compulsory up to the age of ten although pupils in Sutton continued until they were twelve. The records of the Charities contain no references to a School Board and an internet search failed to find any either so one assumes that no Board was established.

In 1902, however, another Education Act, sometimes known as the Balfour Act, was passed and in due course this was to end the administration of the schools by the Municipal Charities but not without considerable resistance from some in the community and disagreement within the Trustees of the

Charities. The Act abolished School Boards and established Local Education Authorities (LEAs) to be responsible for schools, including funding, the employment of teachers and allocation of places. The new authorities were to integrate the voluntary and denominational schools into the system and the move was strongly opposed by non-conformists.

In Sutton Coldfield the Town Council wrote to the Charities and the issues were first discussed at a meeting in February, 1903 although the Trustees had been warned that the transfer of the schools could take a considerable time. At this meeting they resolved that the school houses (school buildings), teachers' dwellings, playgrounds and school furniture be transferred to the Local Education Authority subject to three conditions:

1. The LEA would repay money spent on school extensions.
2. At least one third of the new Education Committee to be elected from outside the Council and two of these to be nominated by the Trustees.
3. That moral and religious instruction be given in the schools "as contemplated by the Scheme of 1817".

Attempts by some of the Trustees to amend clause 2 and omit clause 3 were defeated.

A month later the Trustees resolved to ask the Town Council to join them in an application to the Board of Education for a Compromise Order "allocating three fifths of the net income of the Charity to educational and two fifths to Eleemosynary purposes" (general charitable purposes). Again there was dissension with some of the Trustees wanting a 50:50 split and, very unusually, a vote was demanded. The outcome was that the resolution was carried by 8 votes to 6. Presumably the approach to the Board of Education was made because at the next meeting of the Trustees in May they considered a letter from the Board which dealt with relatively minor matters but there was also an interim Order which recommended that the LEA should group all the schools belonging to the Charities under one body of Managers of whom eight would be appointed by the Trustees and four by the Council. The Trustees promptly objected to being asked to recommend rather than nominate their members on the Education Committee but later withdrew their objection because of possible difficulties with the Council. When they resolved that their representatives should be W.C.H. Brampton and Rev. W.C.R. Bedford (the

Rector) the latter refused because he was recommended and not nominated so he was replaced by J. Ellison. By June 1903 the Managers required by the Board of Education were appointed and Alderman Burman, Rev. W.C.R Bedford, Mr Taylor and Mr Brampton were appointed Foundation managers to represent the Trustees. The latter also considered a resolution from the town Council which agreed to apply for a compromise order "allocating half the net income of the Charities to educational and half to eleemosynary purposes". After three attempts to amend this proposal to different proportions were defeated the Trustees accepted the Council's resolution.

At the same meeting the Trustees agreed on the property to be handed over to the Council as follows:

> Hill School – the school premises and a piece of pasture behind the girls' school, except for a part of the school master and school mistresses' gardens which would be leased to the Trustees of Four Oaks and Hill Village Public Hall.
> Roughley Infants – all the premises.
> Walmley Schools – the premises and a small piece of land.
> Boldmere and Maney Schools – the premises.
> Green Lanes School – the premises and the master's garden.

There is no record of any proposals for the Town Schools at this stage and it was another six months before the Trustees met to discuss the response from the Council and they dealt with Town Schools then. The Council accepted the Trustees' offer but asked them to withdraw their condition that "one third at least of the Education Committee be elected from outside the Council, two of such … to be appointed from time to time on the nomination of the Trustees". The Council proposed to introduce a scheme for moral and religious instruction. Although the minutes of the Trustees' meetings do not record the discussions, this was clearly contentious because a motion for adjournment was carried and the matter was raised at the next meeting in January, 1904. Alderman Burman proposed a motion to accept the terms of the LEA but an amendment was put down by Alderman Crockford and Alderman Glover which accepted the terms but then went on "that in recognition of the fact that for many years past the religious teaching in the schools has been denominational the right to grant the use of such schools and school furniture rent free, for Sunday schools and also for similar denominational religious instruction during the half hour prior to the time appointed for the commencement of secular instruction on not more than three mornings in each week be reserved, the LEA to be entitled to impose reasonable restrictions in order to ensure regularity on the part of teachers and prevent interference with the school for educational purposes". This amendment was lost and the previous motion was carried by 10 votes to 4 with one "neutral" but the reference to religious instruction was a portent of trouble ahead. The motion to transfer schools and land was amended to exclude Town Infants School and playground but the LEA was to be allowed to use this school for seven years at a peppercorn rent.

In May 1904 the Trustees received a letter from the Board of Education which enclosed an appeal from ratepayers against the transfer of schools and informed them that the transfer could not go ahead until there was a response from the LEA. The letter, which was from 505 ratepayers who had heard that the transfer of the schools was to go ahead raised four objections:

> a. In a Scheme of 1825 the schools were established for "the moral and religious instruction of children of the poor inhabitants".
> b. The system, known as Dr. Bell's (see above) had "secured for 80 years definite Church of England teaching in the schools".
> c. The system had "proved to be well suited to the requirements of the district and acceptable to the parents of the scholars".
> d. If the transfer went ahead they would have to conform to the 1870 Education Act which required that "no religious catechism … which is distinctive of any particular denomination shall be taught in the school".

The objectors asked that the present system be continued.

A special meeting was called at which the Trustees considered the objections summarised above and also a paper from the Education Committee of the Town Council which made the following responses:

> The Scheme of 1825 applied to the older schools and included the provisions in points a. and b. above but added that the teaching system could be based upon other plans "which may be thought more eligible." The Bell system "implied no necessary

connection with the teaching of the doctrines of the Church of England or any other denomination." Furthermore, the Master in Chancery had refused to allow the erection of a Chapel of Ease at Hill because the use of funds of the charity for this purpose was not consistent with its "provisions and directions". So, the Council argued, the schools were intended to be non-denominational and, before being taken over by the Municipal Charities in 1886, were designated Corporation Schools. It was also the opinion of the Council that "how and when the teaching of the distinctive doctrines of the Church of England came to be introduced is not known". Perhaps it may have been the result of take-over by the Municipal Charities whose Trustees included three or four Church of England clergymen who played a major part in the administration of the schools.

In response to objection c. above the Council argued that "the Parents and Scholars had no option as there were no other schools" and that the Bell system had ceased to exist. It was also their opinion that "any system involving the teaching of a particular religious doctrine is not likely to prove acceptable to ratepayers in the future."

The Council agreed with the objectors' fourth point that if the schools were transferred "definite Church of England teaching will *ipso facto* cease" but suggested that "this, however, will involve no injustice because the schools in their inception were undenominational, and the Church has never contributed to the funds either for their erection or for their maintenance."

The Trustees approved the report from the Council which was then able to inform the Board of Education that there was complete agreement between the Town Council (the LEA) and the Trustees of the Municipal Charities and that the transfer also had the support of "the great majority of the Burgesses". The Council suggested that "the public interest "demands an immediate settlement of all questions affecting Elementary Education and asked the Board to "receive, at the earliest possible date, a Deputation consisting of the Mayor of the Borough, the Chairman of the Education Committee and the Chairman of the Municipal Charity Trustees to consider the matter." There is no record of any further discussions or the outcome of the delegation to meet the Board but later in the year the Trustees were considering a new scheme which was to deal with the division of income and the school buildings. Some seven months later the Trustees approved a revised Scheme and agreed to the transfer of the schools and the process was complete by the beginning of November 1905.

This new Scheme, which was sealed on 23rd June, 1905, distinguished between the non-educational Charity which was to deal with the various charitable activities of the Charities except for those which became the responsibility of a new educational charity to be known as the Corporation Schools Foundation. This retained ownership of the school buildings, playgrounds and several houses and gardens and some residue of income from the former Corporation Charity. This new Foundation was to be under the jurisdiction of the Board of Education which produced a new Scheme for the purpose and this was sealed on 26th June 1906. It provided for the income to be paid to the Local Education Authority until 31st March 1907 after which it would be held in trust for the Foundation until the Board produced a further Scheme.

A year later the Trustees considered a draft Scheme at several meetings and a final version was sealed on 29th June, 1909. It established that the Corporation Schools Foundation was to be administered by the Trustees of the Corporation Almshouse and Eleemosynary Charity (the remaining part of the Municipal Charities) and set out the procedures for the Trustees such as appointment and the conduct of meetings. It provided that the income up to 31st March was to be paid to the LEA but that after that date it was to be used as follows:

> A yearly sum, not exceeding £165 for gifts of clothing to poor children resident in the borough and in attendance at a public elementary school "having obtained from the Managers of the School a certificate of good conduct, regularity in attendance and progress in learning".
>
> One half of the residue to be accumulated pending a further Scheme for the advancement of Secondary Education.
>
> The other half to be paid to the LEA to be used for grants of up to £5 to pupils remaining at school beyond the leaving age (subject to a total sum of £50) and the remainder for "the support and maintenance of the Public Elementary Schools". So came to an end the direct involvement of the Municipal Charities in the management of local schools and, some twenty years later, the beginning of grant-making.

In the meantime, education is only mentioned twice in the records of the Charities. The first of these, in July 1915, is one of the very few references to World War I which occurred when a Trustee suggested that a grant be made to the Technical School for the purchase of machinery for the engineering class. The Clerk was instructed to apply to the Board of Education for permission to award £100 to "provide lathes, tools etc. to enable the teaching of engineering and the **making of munitions** at the Technical School". It is perhaps not surprising to find that The Trustees were informed in November that the Board would not agree to the use of funds for the establishment of munitions classes.

The second is in a note of a meeting held on 11th January, 1923 when the Trustees asked the Clerk to "request the Town Council as the Local Education Authority to transfer the school and the school house at Roughley to the Trustees" as the buildings had not been used for school purposes for many years. There is no further mention of this school in the minutes of Trustees' meetings until January 1948 when their General Purposes and Estates Committee considered reports from their Clerk and the Town Clerk. Both these were requested following the 1944 Education Act which made Warwickshire County Council the Local Education Authority to take over the schools from the Town Council.

In his report, dated June 1947, the Town Clerk explained the history of the schools and how the Town Council took them over, drawing attention to the phrase "use of schools" being handed over because the Trustees had no powers to hand over the property. In the case of Roughley School the premises were not used as a school after 1909 but no action was taken because the Council thought they may be required later. In about 1938 the idea of re-opening the school was abandoned and it fell into disrepair. In common with other buildings and land connected with schools which were no longer in use as such the Town Clerk stated that the rents collected should be handed back to the Municipal Charities. The Ministry of Education endorsed the agreement on the transfer of school buildings with the County Council in 1954 but it was nearly four years later before the Trustees agreed to repairs being done to the Roughley School House. A note that a new WC Bucket was to be bought for the house illustrates the facilities then available. The house and the school were finally sold in June 1957 and are still occupied.

To go back some years and to the provisions of the 1909 Scheme which established the Corporation Schools Foundation and required half of the income to be accumulated as a fund for "the advancement of Secondary

Education" nothing apparently happened until 1930 when the Trustees began to consult about a draft scheme with other interested parties, including the County Director of Education, the Governors of the two grammar schools and two representative of the elementary schools. In July 1931 the Trustees sent the draft scheme to the Board of Education which, almost a year later, asked for discussions with the Trustees and the County Education Authority. The Board refused to come to Sutton so the discussions took place in London and a new Scheme was accepted by the Trustees in July 1932 and finally sealed on 6th January, 1933 nearly ten years after the Corporation Schools Foundation was established.

The new Scheme first required the payment to the LEA of a contribution towards the cost of providing and equipping Sutton Coldfield Girls High School of £6,250 plus interest of £837. The remainder of the Secondary Education Fund was then to be used in the following ways:

> "a. in assisting pupils to attend schools, universities and other institutions for educational purposes, other than elementary.
>
> b. in other ways promoting education in the Borough of Sutton Coldfield education other than elementary, for which purpose the Trustees may … apply capital endowment as well as income or towards meeting the cost of capital expenditure incurred from time to time at the Sutton Coldfield Grammar School of the Sutton Coldfield High School for Girls." (Clerk's Report 11.1.1946)

Exhibitions were to be awarded to boys or girls who satisfied the Trustees that they were in need of financial assistance and could be for fees or maintenance. They were to be awarded by free and open competition either after an examination or without examination and Trustees were to take into consideration the needs of the candidate, their ability to profit by further education, their school record and any report by the head teacher. The Trustees were also required to consult the LEA and empowered to withdraw the exhibition if the student "is guilty of serious misconduct or idleness, or fails to maintain a reasonable standard of proficiency, or ceases to pursue his education".

In order to administer the Fund the Trustees set up a Secondary Education Fund Committee which comprised six Trustees of whom five were Council representatives. The first meeting was held in July 1934 and grants were awarded to four boys at Bishop Vesey's Grammar School (previously referred to as the Grammar School), two girls at the High School, one at Birmingham School of Art and one at Sutton School of Art, one pupil at King Edward's School, Birmingham and one student at Birmingham University, all for maintenance. They also gave £10 to Sutton Coldfield Technical and Commercial Institute for prizes. Because the results of the Higher School Certificate examinations were not available until August, several application were deferred and the Trustees decided to meet in September in future years and also later in the year to consider grants which had been awarded in instalments or were to be renewed.

The minutes of most of the meetings record the awards made but occasionally there is a little more information which throws some light on the social conditions at the time. In 1936 a grant was made to a girl at the High School for a mid-day meal, books, boots and clothing for £10 a year for three years. A grant was made to a girl from Princess Alice Orphanage who was also supported by the orphanage in 1942 and at the same meeting an award was made to the child of an assistant master at the Bishop Vesey's Grammar School whose annual salary was £590. Three sisters who attended the High School received maintenance awards whilst at school and then at college.

The first of the very few references to the Second World War was in May 1940 when the full Board went into committee to discuss the report from the Secondary Education Committee. This appears to have been a device to exclude any members of the press or public who may have been present because the agenda involved confidential or sensitive issues. The committee recommended seven awards, including a renewal and two increases and these were approved by the Board. Another recommendation was to renew a grant to a very able student at Cambridge who had been awarded a first in part 1 of his degree and also a prize. The Board refused to make this award on hearing that the young man was a Conscientious Objector and also withdrew another grant to "a youth at Cambridge" who had left to join a Friends Ambulance Unit. At their next meeting they went further and, having withdrawn a grant of £60 to a fourth year student who was a Conscientious Objector they resolved that no future applications from Conscientious Objectors would be considered and that any already made would be withdrawn. This policy continued until 26th September

1946 which was, of course, after the end of the war but during the period of compulsory National Service. Later in 1940 they also stopped a grant to a Cambridge student who had registered with the forces.

In 1943, two grants were discontinued when the women recipients joined the forces and the final references to the war occurred in January 1945 when a girl who was awarded her chemistry degree after only two years instead of three, had to leave because of National Service regulations and went to work as a research chemist at Billingham. At the same meeting it is noted that a girl on a three year teaching course had to leave after two years and start work because of a teacher shortage. An award was also made to a student to read engineering at Birmingham University although his qualifications seem to have been only seven subjects in School Certificate. In 1946, a year after the war ended, a student who failed in his first year and therefore lost his award said that he planned to continue his studies in Czechoslovakia. My last example of a unique case is that of a student leaving Bishop Vesey's Grammar School in 1947 who was given a grant for a medical course at Birmingham University. After a successful career as General Practitioner in Sutton Coldfield, Dr. N.F.D. Cooper became a Trustee of the Municipal Charities in 1989 and later served as Chairman for three years.

In 1944 the Butler Education Act revolutionised the education system and, in particular placed new responsibilities upon Local Education Authorities for providing financial support for students in higher and further education. The new arrangements would clearly affect the provision of grants by the Municipal Charities and the Chairman and the Clerk held a meeting with the Education Officer responsible for the Division which included Sutton Coldfield to clarify their responsibilities. Unfortunately, the outcome of their discussions is not recorded. During the next year the Charities continued to make grants and only one problem is recorded: the Local Authority (Warwickshire County Council) reduced a student's grant by the amount awarded by the Charities and the Clerk was asked to "sort it out". In October 1948 the Trustees sent all the renewals and new applications to the LEA because, they argued, it was the LEA's responsibility. However, it was not that simple because a month later they were having to consider each case individually to sort out the responsibilities of the Charities, the LEA and, in some cases, the Ministry of Education. After this there are no further references to awards for students who had left school and meetings were dominated by two further effects of the 1944 Act viz. the future of school buildings and the sharing of funds between the Charities and the Town Council.

In June 1947 the Town Clerk wrote a report for the Council about the transfer of school premises under Section 6 of the 1944 Education Act and revealed a complicated situation. Apart from the schools which were originally run by the Municipal Charities there were ten others. One of these, New Oscott Infants School, had been managed by the committee of the National Children's Home and Orphanage until 1930 when the Council agreed to manage the school for five years. Although the agreement was never renewed, the Council continued its management. All the others had to be dealt with individually because some were built by the Council on its own land, some were built on land intended for housing and some encroached on land belonging to other bodies. Each one was transferred to the new LEA, the County Council, but in some cases the lease of the land was retained. One school, St Joseph's was a voluntary Roman Catholic school so no question of transfer arose and the school still flourishes, albeit in more modern buildings. The remaining twelve schools which had been handed over to the Town Council by the Municipal Charities in 1902 were listed as Town Girls, Town Infants (formerly Town Boys), Hill Boys, Hills Girls, Hill Infants, Maney Infants, Walmley Infants, Walmley Mixed, Green Lanes Junior Mixed, Green Lanes Infants, Boldmere Girls, Boldmere Infants and the Town Clerk referred to the Minutes of the Charities for 1902 when the Trustees agreed to "hand over the use of the schools" to the Council because they had no power to dispose of their property. The schools became "provided schools" which apparently relieved the Charities from any responsibility for maintaining the fabric of the buildings as long as they were in use by the Council. The Town Clerk further reported that "the corporation had only the right to use these schools as they then stood, and that when they ceased to be used as schools they reverted, or will revert to the Trustees of the Municipal Charities."

Inevitably, there were complications relating to particular schools. Victoria Road Boys School and the Trinity Hill Handicrafts Centre were erected by the Council but on land belonging to the Charities and were treated as the schools listed above. The Boldmere schools, built by the Corporation, infringed on land owned by the Charities, including part of the old Boldmere Girls School which was in use as an ambulance depot and which should have reverted to the Charities when it ceased to be used as a school. Therefore the rent paid to the Council should be given to the Charities.

The Council ceased to use Boldmere Infants School in October 1938 but it was not handed back to the Charities. After remaining empty until December 1939 it was then used as a Child Welfare Clinic until October 1942. Once again it remained empty until 21st September 1943 when the Council spent "a fairly large sum of money" on adapting the building for use as a school meals kitchen and the Town Clerk suggested that there should be negotiations with the Trustees to permit its continued use and, presumably, the payment of an appropriate rent. The report also dealt with Roughley School (see above) and suggested that the former Charities schools should be handed over to the County Council as the new Education Authority "on their undertaking to notify the Trustees of the Municipal Charities immediately they cease to use the schools as such, and to return the documents to the Trustees." In January 1948 the General Purposes and Estates Committee of the Charities discussed the Town Clerk's report, particularly in relation to Roughley and Boldmere but it was another nine years before they sold the buildings at Roughley and Boldmere is not mentioned again. The matter was finally resolved by an agreement signed on 4th November by all the Trustees of the Municipal Charities and the Clerk to the County Council and authorised by the Minister of Education. This identified each school precisely and divided them into two groups. The first comprised the former Boldmere Girls School and Boldmere Infants School which were then partly included in the site of the Boldmere Secondary School and to which the Trustees agreed to "waive any claim which they might have to the property" and further confirmed the absolute title of the County Council from 1st April 1945.

The second part comprised the following schools:

Title in 1953	Previous Description
Town County Primary	Town Boys (later Town Infants and Girls Schools
Town County Primary	Two Playgrounds and a garden
Hill County Junior and Infants	Hill Boys and Hill Girls
Teacher Centre	Hill Infants
Maney County Infants	Maney Infants
Walmley County	Walmley Infants and Mixed
Wylde Green Primary	Green Lanes Junior and Infants.

For these schools the County Council waived any claim to them and admitted the title of the Trustees of the Charities. The County Council were to use the buildings rent free but be responsible for all outgoings and they were to use them for educational purposes i.e. schools for any ages, youth clubs and occasional evening lettings. On ceasing to use them for any of these purposes the Council were required to return them to the Trustees, having notified them within one month.

A notable omission from these negotiations was the Duke Street School which was not returned to the Trustees until 1973.

The other major impact of the 1944 Education Act was upon the disposal of the income of the School Education Fund, half of which (one quarter of the total income of the Charities after the payment of administrative costs) had been paid to the Borough Council as the Local Education Authority. Although this responsibility was passed to Warwickshire County Council by the Act the payments from the Charities were retained by the Borough Council and there is no mention of them until 1961 when some of the Trustees and representatives of the Council met to consider their position under the 1944 Act. Apparently the payments to the Council had accumulated to over £16,000 and were increasing by over £1,000 a year. It was agreed that two thirds of the income of the Charities should be used for the general charitable activities such as the maintenance of the almshouses, provision of blankets etc. and the other third to go to the School Education fund. Of this, half would be used for grants to students and the other half would be paid to the Council to be used for additional educational functions. This money was to be kept separate from other revenue and used for special projects such as grants for libraries, equipment, school swimming baths and a youth centre. This would have required a new Scheme from the Charity Commissioners and is not mentioned again. However, in 1965 it became clear that money was still being paid to the Borough Council when it was reported to the Trustees that the total amount accumulated by the Council since 1944 had reached £27,000 and that a sub-committee of seven Councillors, one Trustee and a representative of a head teachers' association had been set up to consider its use. Heads were to submit written requests for grants or loans and the subcommittee was to specify the objects of the awards. Nothing further seems to have happened and there is no record of such awards.

Three years later a new Scheme from the Charity Commissioners excludes any reference to the School Education Fund but, for the first time, specified the ways in which the General Charity should pursue the object of "advancement of education":

(a) Awards for fees and maintenance at schools, colleges or
    universities approved by the Trustees.

(b) Financial assistance, clothing, tools, instruments or books to help those leaving educational establishments to enter a profession or trade.

(c) The promotion of education in Sutton Coldfield in other ways.

The Trustees were allowed to make rules "as to the value and tenure of scholarships and the method of selecting candidates". Two conditions were to apply: the beneficiaries were to be under twenty five and to have lived in Sutton Coldfield for at least five years immediately before the award was made. Thus the distinction between this aspect of the General Charity and the School Education Fund largely disappeared and remained only to complicate the work of the accountant to the Trustees. In 1965 the Trustees had discussed a draft of this Scheme and had expected the School Education Fund to be subsumed into the General Charity but presumably the Commissioners were not prepared to agree.

The minutes of the Trustees' meetings do not record the fate of the funds held by the Borough Council but some twenty years later, in the course of a talk given to the Trustees, the Clerk said that the result of a meeting between Warwickshire County Council, Sutton Borough Council and the Trustees in 1978 was that the money was returned to the Charities and became a major part of School Education Fund's capital which then (probably about 1990) amounted to £36,000.

Meanwhile, the policy on grants was beginning to change in response to these developments. In the summer of 1964 the Trustees sought the approval of the Ministry of Education for a grant of £1,000 from the Secondary Education Fund to Warwick University in response to its appeal. Approval was given early in the following year and another grant of £500 was made in 1969. In 1972 the individual grants included one to a boy who had won a scholarship to Rugby School and whose mother was a widow and, two years later, a similar award was made to a pupil at Chetham's School in Manchester. In 1976 the first grants to educational organisations were being made and included awards to five primary schools, a school music association and a sports association. Six months later grants ranging from £62 to £600 were made to five primary schools, Bishop Walsh Secondary School and the Teachers' Centre and this set the pattern for future years. Where the purposes of the grants were mentioned in the minutes of the meetings they included curtains, furnishings and camping equipment but a request for examination fees was refused. Another development occurred in 1980 when an interest free loan was given to Whitehouse Common Middle School, repayable at £25 a month, towards the cost of a swimming pool. This was another example of the way in which the interpretation of the responsibilities of the LEA was evolving because, twenty years earlier, an identical request from Fairfax School for help with the cost of a swimming pool was refused on the grounds that it was an LEA responsibility. Later in 1980 a loan of £1,500 was made to Longmoor Special School for £1,500, with repayments of £35 a month, for a minibus garage. Occasional similar loans were made to other schools but after about ten years the Trustees discontinued the practice in favour of making the more substantial grants which became possible after the criteria for making educational awards from the General Charity was clarified and as their disposable income increased considerably. Grants were made in response to requests from individuals or schools and previous awards and the nature of the request were taken into account by the Trustees. They received details of the request, information about the school, including the number of pupils and their ages and a list of previous awards.

As the number and size of the awards was increasing more and more of them were made from the General Charity so it became a nuisance and somewhat confusing to allocate the applications to this fund or to the School Education Fund, each of which was required to have separate accounts, so in 1990 the Clerk began to investigate the possibility of combining them. This was pursued by the new Clerk from 1991 but there was resistance from the Charity Commissioners and nothing changed until a new Charity Act in 1993 allowed the accounts to be combined although separate records and books still had to be kept. As a result very few grants were made from the School Education Fund but in 1997 it was found that it had been established from income and had no endowments or capital. It was suggested that if grants were made from the Fund until it was used up it might then be closed and when this was put to the Commissioners they agreed. There were requests for large grants from two of the secondary schools and the Trustees awarded £94,500 to Arthur Terry School for Information Technology equipment and £98,000 to Sutton Girl' School for the refurbishment of the Food Technology rooms and the tennis courts. At their meeting on 1st May 1998, the Trustees agreed to pay these awards from the School Education Fund thus using up all its money. In a letter dated 2nd July 1998 the Charity Commissioners accepted the closure of the School Education Fund and it was removed from the Central Register of

Charities. Since then all grants for educational purposes have been made from the General Charity.

In the same year there were also large grants to Fairfax School which received £90,000 towards the extension of the school hall, £90,000 to Plantsbrook School towards improved science facilities and £75,000 to Bishop Vesey's Grammar School towards a new sports hall. When grants to schools were first made they were for "providing such special benefits of any kind not normally provided by the local education authority" (the 1982 Scheme) but as the cost of new equipment increased and the authority was unable to provide for all the needs of the schools so the grants were increased to provide both equipment and buildings. Some of the larger awards to secondary schools were made to assist their applications for Specialist College status for which they needed to raise funds which were then matched by government grants.

Meanwhile, grants to primary schools, especially for information technology equipment and library improvements, were increased in proportion to the numbers of pupils and in 1998-9 for example, which was a typical year, there were seven awards of between £10,000 and £23,000 as well as several smaller ones. By 2005-6 the largest grant to a primary school had reached almost £28,000.

Grants to individual students also seem to have reflected the changing circumstances caused by new regulations affecting government grants, student loans and, most recently, the return of fees. In 1997-8 twenty three students received grants of from £38 to £2,200 totalling £16,510. In the following year the number of grants fell to nine and the trend continued until 2002-3 when one student was awarded £3,000. In 2005-6 there were fourteen grants amounting to £7,500.

The involvement of the Sutton Coldfield Municipal Charities in education continued the management of schools begun by the Warden and Society until the very early twentieth century when they were returned to the Borough Council. Since then they have supported individual students, although the arrangements for payment of fees and maintenance grants by the local authority at the time have changed the need for additional help. Support for schools, which began with relatively small amounts for "extras" such as hall curtains, sports equipment and loans towards the installation of swimming pools, has increased enormously and has played a major part in improving the facilities available to the children attending Sutton Coldfield schools. (See Chapter 8)

Chapter 7

PROPERTY, LAND
AND INVESTMENTS

THE GENERAL records of the Municipal Charities tend to include references to the properties only when there was a change of tenancy or a sale and when there was a need for repairs and maintenance so it is not possible to trace the fate of all of them without a detailed study of those deeds which are available and of period maps. Such detailed investigation is beyond the scope of this book so the information in this chapter is derived largely from the minutes of the meetings of the Trustees.

The growth in income which enabled the Trustees to increase grants towards the end of the twentieth century was very largely the result of increased land and property values and especially of the demand for both as a result of the growth and development of the town. Vastly increased rents and the re-investment of the proceeds of land and property sales provided an income which the first Trustees would never have imagined and which transformed the philanthropic activities of the Municipal Charities. So how did the Charities obtain this critical source of capital?

When Sutton Coldfield eventually became a Municipal Borough in 1886 the Scheme of the Privy Council laid down that "All property of any kind whatsoever … possessed by or vested in the Old Corporation … which property is within the meaning of Section 4 of the Municipal Corporations Act 1883, is applicable to charity or defined charitable purposes vested in … the 'Trustees of Municipal Charities in the Borough of Sutton Coldfield' jointly by them to be applied in the manner in which and for the purposes for which such property, or the income thereof, was before the passing of that Act applicable". Those Trustees were Rev. William Campbell Riland Bedford, Allen Lepard Crockford, Henry Duncalf, Thomas Hayward, George Lowe, Rev. Albert Smith,

Samuel Allen Taylor and Rev. Montague Webster who were the first co-optative Trustees of the Municipal Charities. Thus the charitable duties and resources of the Old Corporation (the Warden and Society) were separated from the new corporation and became the responsibility of the new Municipal Charities.

The Scheme sealed in January 1898 includes a schedule of all the properties and shares owned by the Municipal Charities. There were one hundred parcels of land, some of which included houses and gardens, producing an annual gross income of over £722 with individual rents ranging from two shillings and sixpence (about twelve pence) for a garden in Church Hill to £140 18s 6d for property in Tudor Hill. In addition the Charities owned twenty almshouses and nine schools and the houses and gardens for the Mistresses and Masters of the schools. The shares, mostly consuls bought on the instructions of the Chancery Division of the High Court after the improper sale of timber from Sutton Park early in the nineteenth century, were valued at over £22,290 and produced a gross annual income of £850. Dividends from two investments were left to accumulate. The Lord's Meadow Charity and the Charity of Thomas Jesson also owned a small quantity of land and shares producing an annual gross income of £36 and £17 respectively.

The first reference to the acquisition of additional property occurs in 1900 when the Trustees agreed to purchase ground rents of property in Selly Oak, Birmingham, partly with the surplus of the Lingard bequest after the erection of the two almshouses. It was also planned to use for this purpose an additional £500 received from the sale of a piece of land adjoining Walmley Vicarage to the Trustees of Queen Anne's Bounty (a charity for assisting with the provision and furnishing of dwellings for clergy) but the Charity Commissioners required the Trustees to invest this money, in the name of the Trustee of Charitable Funds, in Consuls. The Selly Oak property was also the first of several purchases out side the Borough of Sutton Coldfield.

In 1901 trees were felled in Manorial Woods and £70 from the proceeds was used to plant new ones. These woods are still owned and maintained by the Charities. The land on which stands the Horse and Jockey hotel is also still part of the Charities' property and is first mentioned in July 1896 when Ansells Brewery applied for a 99 year lease and were refused.

Negotiations continued, with references to road widening, and in 1903 the Trustees approved plans to extend the Hotel but the agreement on the lease was not reached until 1910. In 1936 this lease was surrendered and a new one for seventy years was agreed at a ground rent of £130 a year and the tenants

The Horse and Jockey pub on the corner of Jockey Road and Birmingham Road, circa 1900.

The Horse and Jockey pub 1892.

The Cup pub c.1890. Mrs Ellery was the landlady. This building was demolished in 1893.

undertook to carry out repairs and improvements to the value of £4,000 over the first three years. A year later there was a request from Mitchells and Butlers, who leased the other public house owned by the Charities, and they surrendered their lease in November 1937. They were granted a new one for seventy years on condition that they spent at least £2,500 on alterations.

In May 1906 the Trustees agreed to lease out 1,350 square yards of land at Mere Green on the corner of Lichfield Road and Mere Green Road and paid £1 in compensation to the school master (George Field) who had used it as a garden. Shops with living accommodation were built on this land but now that the leases are due to expire proposals for the development of this and adjoining land are under active consideration, and the land sold to a developer.

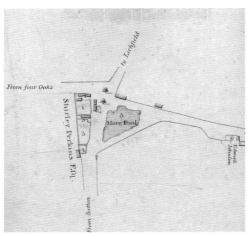

Sketch map of Mere Green.

In January 1911 the Surveyor was asked to prepare a report on the condition of the various properties and the Trustees arranged to carry out an inspection which became established as a tradition that continued until very recently. The first inspection took place on the second of June 1911 and a car was hired at a cost of £2. In the early days and certainly up to 1961 almost all the decisions about maintenance were taken only after the inspection but in recent years the Surveyor has reported regularly to the Trustees and decisions have been taken by the Management Committee which met every two months unless there were special meetings to deal with specific issues. Annual Inspections now may be to look at properties, proposed developments or to see the outcome of grants made to organisations such as churches, schools and clubs or associations.

In May 1913 the Surveyor reported to the General Purposes Committee of the Trustees that all the authorised repairs had been carried out and that "all farms, cottages and other buildings are now in good condition". However, his comments were, of course, relative to conditions at the time and some properties were without mains water or sewerage connections.

There are few references to the First World War in the minutes of the meetings of the Charities but it is recorded that the tenant of Hill Hook Farm and Mill applied for a rent reduction because he was serving in the army and was refused because he was receiving an allowance from "the Civil Liberties Commission". In 1918 the Trustees agreed to the "breaking up of some land at Blake Street in the occupation of Higgins" and some more in Walmley, both at the request of the Warwickshire War Agricultural Committee. In April 1920 the Trustees agreed to the erection of a War Memorial "on land in front of the almshouses on condition that a sufficient sum be set aside by the Memorial Committee to provide for the proper maintenance of the Memorial". Since then it has been the focus for a parade service in November each year and was removed to a new and less dangerous site recently.

A significant development began in July 1921 when a parcel of land in Green Lanes, Wylde Green was leased to Mr W J Davies who was to expend not less than £1,800 on three pairs of houses. This was the first of a series of similar transactions. Mr Davies leased four more plots in the following year and two more a few months later, with another lease being granted to Mr Cox. In 1923 several more leases were granted to Mr Davies and land in Penns Lane was also leased out for building. This was the start of housing developments on Charities' land which have continued until recently, although the later transactions have involved the sale of land and re-investment of the proceeds.

Not all the land leased was used for building and a field off Tamworth Road, adjoining the railway, was leased for seven years initially from May 1924 to the Congregational Church for use as a sports field. Later it was used jointly by the United Reformed Church, the successor to the Congregational Church, and the Methodist Church. The field still continues to be used for tennis and cricket although the committee which leases it is no longer church based.

Some of the property owned by the Charities was very old and caused problems for the Trustees. Woodbine Cottage in Ox Leys Road was inspected in 1929 and found to be too dilapidated to repair so it was pulled down. Water and sanitation problems occurred with some of the other properties and on several occasions improvements were made in response to pressure from the local authority. At Barn Farm in Lindridge Road, for example, work was done in 1933 when alterations were required by the "Sanitary Authority". After the Surveyor told the Trustees in 1934 that the Medical Officer of Health was not satisfied with the condition of the water supply at Manorial Farm a new well was dug and fitted with a pump and cover at a cost of £30 8 0 and eleven years later a water supply was installed at Manorial Cottages in Worcester Lane in response to pressure from the Council. However, problems here continued and, two years afterwards, the Surveyor was asked to consult with the Medical Officer of Health about the cottages. Nearly ten years after the end of the Second World War, in May 1955 after the death of the tenant, the Trustees agreed to purchase "a new WC bucket" for Roughley School House so presumably there was still no connection to sewers at that time. During this period when properties were slowly being brought up to more modern standards another aspect of water supply was raised and there is a note that the water to a trough at the corner of Park Drive and Four Oaks Drive was to be disconnected. Presumably because of a decline in horse traffic in Four Oaks!

Progress towards present day standards was slow and although a bathroom and WC were installed at Wharton's Farm (Biddles Farm) in 1947, it was not until April 1966 that it was agreed that a bedroom at Manorial Farm should be converted into its first bathroom. Two months later the Council served a notice that houses in Riland Road belonging to the Charities were without standard

Manorial Farm. The farm is still owned by the Charities and is let to a tenant who also has livery stables and lives in the house.

amenities and the Trustees hurriedly called a meeting with their Surveyor but there is no record of action taken. Apparently, this pattern of a reactive approach to maintenance continued because in January 1969 there was a report from the Medical Officer of Health that Oak Cottage was unfit for habitation and that he would seek a demolition order if appropriate repairs were not carried out. The Trustees instructed the Surveyor to prepare a scheme of work and to submit it to the Borough's Health and Welfare Committee. Six months later the Trustees approved remedial work costing up to £2,000 and applied for a grant towards this amount. Almost immediately after this the Medical Officer was expressing concern about the state of another property, Springfield Farm, and he was still doing so in January 1971. It seems that the Charities applied for planning permission to rebuild the farm and it was refused because it is recorded that, after the Trustees inspected the property in June 1972, the Planning Authority was asked to reconsider its decision. As the farmhouse is still in use today, although alterations have been made, the appeal must have been unsuccessful.

In November, 1942 the first reference to Hill Hook Mill shows that the lease was surrendered and in the following January it was agreed that the tenancy should be advertised. Later that year the Trustees decided to appoint a solicitor to "gain possession of various hutments at Hill Hook Mill" including those used by weekenders. About a year later it is recorded that the number of hutments was reduced from 21 to 14 and, in July 1943, when a new tenancy was approved, proceedings were begun against the remaining weekenders with huts. By May 1944 three weekend huts and six permanent dwellings were left at the mill and a year later work began on an additional cesspit. At this time four buildings remained so a notice for their removal was served and approval was given to begin court proceeding if they were not removed. At this stage there is one of the relatively few references to the Second World War because a letter was received from the Officer Commanding the Legal Aid Section of the "British Liberation Army" about a service wife and two children living at Hill Hook and all notices to quit were withdrawn. In May 1946 another building was vacated leaving two families and the Trustees tried to get them rehoused by the neighbouring City of Birmingham. The outcome is not recorded but later that year a Mr G Harrison was granted a one year lease for agricultural purposes only. In January 1947 the Trustees decided to give first refusal to the Corporation if they decided to sell the mill but is was not put up for sale until February 1956 after the tenant died. There are no more references to the mill and its pool but the latter, together with a small garden area incorporating a millstone and cog wheel, now form part of the Hill Hook Mill Nature Reserve which is managed by Birmingham City Council.

In January, 1961 an additional purpose for farm land was found when the Corporation applied for its use for tipping rubbish (landfill) at a field in Hillwood Road which is part of Manorial Farm and also on Land off Withy Hill Road. Three years later the site at Manorial Farm was extended and tipping continued until 1967 when the Borough Surveyor was asked to reinstate the land used. These fields are now under cultivation although some additional drainage had to be installed in the 1990s. Tipping at Withy Hill continued at least until 1971 when the agreement with the Corporation was extended but there is no record of the closure of the site. Ironically, throughout this period and ever since there has been a spasmodic problem with the illegal dumping of rubbish at Manorial Woods which are on the Camp Lane boundary of Manorial Farm. In September 1965 the Council complained to the Trustees about the rubbish and in June 1969 the minutes of a Board meeting record that they agreed to make a donation to some local Venture Scouts who were going to clear up the rubbish which had accumulated again. The problem continued and in June 1971 the police were asked to keep the woods under observation to prevent dumping. The outcome is not recorded but the dumping of rubbish continues to the present day.

As Sutton Coldfield expanded in the post war period with many new housing developments, the Mere Green crossroads became more significant as a small shopping centre. At this time the Trustees owned a large area of land and several buildings so in January 1962 they set up a sub-committee to consider the whole of their properties in this area. These comprised four almshouses, a Gospel Hall with a small frontage and an area of 178 square yards, Hill Rovers Club Room and land at the rear of the Gospel Hall, an adjoining Scout Hut behind the almshouses and the schools. They also owned adjacent land on which there were shops and living accommodation. Three years previously they had begun to negotiate the sale of the freehold of a block of properties known as The Primroses round the corner in Lichfield Road but ran into trouble with the Charity Commissioners who insisted on notices seeking higher offers for the leases which would not expire until March 1991. The offer price had been £2,050 which invested at 5% would yield £9,750 by the end of the lease but when the Commissioners insisted on a surveyor's report he valued it at £7,500 when the leases ran out and suggested that the offer be accepted. Two months later the Trustees decided to take no action. Nothing further seems to have happened until June 1968 when the Trustees decided to negotiate the freehold of The Primroses and to consider the future of a school. In September they agreed to sell The Primroses, 298-318 Lichfield Road, to a local developer, Ashworth and Stewart, for £12,500.

As the Local Education Authority built new schools and the old buildings were no longer required for educational purposes they began to revert to the Charities and, in September 1972, the Trustees were informed that one of the schools at Mere Green would be returned to them in April 1973. Warwickshire County Council wanted to buy some of the land to build a health centre but was refused. Early in 1973 the sale of a strip of land giving access to a car park was considered but, fortunately as it later turned out when extensive development was considered, the land was licensed to the Council which found itself not owning either of the two access routes to the car park. In June 1974 a small working party was set up to consider all the school sites and a few months later, after consulting the architect, they proposed that 21 shops with living accommodation above should be built on the school sites at Mere Green. By this time Sutton Coldfield was part of Birmingham and its Planning Department asked for amended proposals because, it suggested, that there were already enough shops in the area. Nevertheless, a planning application was submitted in April 1975 and rejected by the Council which also placed a Preservation Order on one of the schools which had been built in 1874. This was followed, a year later, by a Building Preservation Order from the Secretary of State.

Meanwhile, the Trustees agreed to license to Safeways, a supermarket, which now occupied one of the shops built where The Primroses stood, a piece of land for use as a car park if they demolished the remaining buildings, which included a school and a caretaker's house, and erected fencing, subject to planning permission. No fencing appears to have been put up but there was a fairly formidable hedge along the boundary with Lichfield Road where the fence was supposed to be. The original licence was for five years with a reduced rent for the first six months. Since then the shop has been occupied by Kwiksave and now by Somerfield.

The 1874 school building became a bank and part was licensed to "Chantelle" in 1977 as a small retail outlet for five years at £100 a year. Two years later the part occupied by the bank became a restaurant and in 1985 the shop closed and the rooms became part of the restaurant. Since then the building has been refurbished several times and has been a wine bar/restaurant, a seafood restaurant and, most recently, a pub/restaurant (The Old Speckled Hen). One of the other school buildings remained in use as St Joseph's Primary School, then a teachers' centre and finally as a youth and community centre. At the beginning of the new century and after extensive negotiations between the Charities, the City Council and Sainsburys the building was demolished and incorporated into the car park for Sainsburys, the library was demolished and a new library and community centre built. Plans to develop the site of the former library and the remaining properties, including part of the supermarket car park, or to offer the properties for sale were being considered but eventually, the Trustees decided to sell all their land and buildings at Mere Green and the transaction was completed in 2006. Sadly, the developer ran into financial problems, after giving tenants notice and most of the shops are now boarded up until a new owner is found.

As the other schools were replaced by new buildings and the old ones were returned to the Charities they were put to a variety of uses. In September, 1973 the Walmley Junior and Infant school building was handed back and has since been used by several community groups and soon after, in November, the Duke Street School building was returned. At this time the Corporation was working on development plans and considering compulsory purchase but, with local government reorganisation due six months later, did not proceed. Enquiries about use of the school had been received from the Trinity Playgroup and they were granted a licence for five years at an annual rent of £1,200 against which they were awarded a grant of £900. The playgroup is still using the school and the Charities have helped with maintenance costs and have increased the grant as annual rents have increased.

In the centre of the town the very extensive buildings of the Town Schools were the subject of discussions with the Council in 1980, the latter wishing to use them for "educational and multi-purpose social accommodation" but the Trustees would not agree to educational use. Eventually, in 1982, the buildings were offered for sale and bought for £150,000 by the Baptist Church which sold its premises across the road to McDonald's and converted one of the school buildings into a church, with the others being refurbished for various activities. The only school which was retained by the Local Authority is at Wylde Green where there are no plans for a replacement building.

When the Municipal Charities were set up they inherited considerable areas of land on much of which there were dwellings and some other buildings. After the First World War they began to lease more and more land for building and so, by 1967 when the Leasehold Reform Act was passed, they had extensive areas of housing to which it would apply. The Act was considered at the Board meeting in January 1968 and since then, as they became enfranchised, many freeholds have been purchased by homeowners. However a major change of direction began in 1980 with the sale of an extensive area of land at Blake Street on the Northern Boundary of Sutton Coldfield for housing development, to be followed in 1985 by the sale of another large area at nearby Hill Hook. Unfortunately, the discussions of the Trustees at this time are not recorded but it seems reasonable to suggest that their decision at about the same time to begin to purchase large properties elsewhere was to replace those which had been sold with others which would give a good financial return. The first of these was retail and office premises in New Broadway, Ealing, London which was leased to the Automobile Association. Six months later they bought a block of shops, including the supermarket, at Mere Green for £825,000. This was part of the development on land which they sold in 1968. In April 1984 two office buildings in Knowle, to the south of Birmingham, were bought and, at the same meeting, the Board also agreed to spend £455,000 on a farm at Weobley in Herefordshire. This had a house of great historical importance which was built just before Sutton Coldfield received its Charter from which the charitable functions of the Municipal Charities are derived. It is also a very well run commercial undertaking. The last of this group of major purchases was in 1990 when the Board decided to buy two units in a new development, Emmanuel Court, in the centre of Sutton Coldfield for just over one million pounds. Although this proved to be the least productive of all these new acquisitions it marked a move into a new sphere as the number of properties decreased but the capital value and returns were considerably greater.

Buildings and land account for about a third of the Charities' capital base and are now managed by professional surveyors under the watchful eyes of the Trustees. Improved resources and a more modern approach to the property now mean that the Charities are a good landlord with high standards of property maintenance.

Chapter 8

GRANTS TO THE PEOPLE OF SUTTON COLDFIELD

WHEN THE Sutton Coldfield Municipal Charities were established the Trustees were required to continue with the relief of the poor inhabitants of the town which began with the Charter of Henry VIII in 1528. It was reported in 1855 that the benefits provided by the Warden and Society included the provision of linen and the services of a doctor for women in childbirth, the schools, clothing for children, apprenticeships, marriage portions, blankets, almshouses, allowances or pensions and 30 hundredweight of coal for each of the almshouse residents. Some of these awards were originally given by individual charities such as the Poor Maidens' Portions and Jesson's Charity but were controlled by the same Trustees. This chapter will be concerned with grants and pensions made from the General Charity and which began on a fairly small scale but grew rapidly towards the end of the twentieth century and now make a very significant contribution to many individuals and organisations in Sutton Coldfield.

The first available direct reference to grants is in the minutes of a meeting of Trustees in 1894 when they distributed blankets at a cost of £14. 13.9, clothing for school children (£16. 4. 0) and girls' hats (£6. 6. 0). One of the Trustees was responsible for choosing the blankets and a list of applicants was considered by all the Trustees. Presumably, similar awards were made each year but the next reference to them is for 1899 when 20 pairs of blankets at twelve shillings a pair were given out to applicants whose name on a list had been approved. The criteria for choosing them are not disclosed and blankets are rarely mentioned until 1910 when it is recorded that they were "awarded as usual". By 1912 it appears that 49 blankets were given to those selected from 149 applicants and the practice continued until November 1917 when none was awarded because of a government request not to buy blankets where avoidable. The Trustees set aside £17 for the following year but in November 1918, two days before the armistice was declared, the Trustees asked the Mayor (a long-standing Trustee, Alderman Seal) to investigate because blankets were "difficult to obtain at anything like reasonable prices". He must have been successful because a payment of £51. 11. 3 to Mrs Seal for blankets was approved. By 1922 the price had dropped and the Trustees bought 50 blankets at 28 shillings a pair, making a total of £35. 0. 0. For reasons which are not given, in the following year they bought 25 blankets at 25 shillings a pair and another 25 at 30 shillings a pair and there were 129 applicants, Each year a blanket was formally handed to each of the successful applicants, usually about 47, at 10 am on the designated day. Presumably the remaining two or three blankets each year were kept for emergencies.

In 1928 it was decided that a blanket recipient would have to wait a minimum of five years before being eligible for another. The annual distribution of blankets continued in November or December each year but the number of applications was smaller and down to 53 in 1936. There were difficulties in 1939, after the beginning of the Second World War when no blankets were obtainable because of the demand for H.M. Forces but the Trustees were able to distribute some early in 1940. There is another reference to the war in 1944 when permission to purchase blankets had to be obtained from the Wool Control Board and they were not available until January 1945 when there were 71 applicants. By 1948 there were 115 applicants, although only 44 were awarded, and in January 1951, as part of a general reduction in grants the Trustees decided to limit expenditure on blankets to £50. A few months later, on learning that the price of blankets had risen from £1. 11. 7 to £3. 5. 9 they agreed to purchase only 15, at which one of the Trustees, Alderman Busby, decided to buy 5 more himself. The same limit continued from year to year but the price must have varied quite considerably because the number supplied varied from 32 in 1958 to 73 in 1962 from the same source. In that year a blanket was given to each almshouse resident and to 29 out of the other 30 applicants. In 1968 the £50 only bought 20 blankets so £75 was allocated in the following year to buy 30 blankets but only 22 were awarded although there were thirty applicants. The remainder were kept for a later distribution. The allocation was increased to £100 in 1973 and this purchased 50 blankets of which 31 were granted to 31 of the 37 applicants. Two years later only 12 were awarded, at the discretion of one of the Trustees and, as there is no further mention of blankets, we must assume that this was the last distribution, although there is no record of the decision to discontinue the practice.

Throughout the same period the residents of the almshouses were provided with an annual delivery of coal sometimes from local merchants and sometimes directly from a colliery such as the one at Cannock. This was such a routine matter that there are few references to it but it seems that local suppliers were invited to submit tenders and one of the Trustees was appointed to select the successful one. In 1961 two tenders were received and the contract was awarded to F W Hall of Four Oaks Wharf at £7. 13. 6 per ton. Eight years later, the coal was supplied by Jones of Wishaw at £12. 10. 0 per ton. The distribution appears to have been at the rate of one ton per almshouse and to have taken place around Christmas time. In 1971 there were no tenders so the Clerk was authorised to order from a local supplier. There was one further order in 1972 and this seems to have been the last as electric storage heaters were installed in the almshouses.

Whereas the original Scheme had simply directed that the balance of income after the proper management of the charities was to be applied "in accordance with the subsisting trusts" the one sealed in 1905 was rather more specific and included the provision that:

> "There shall be paid to each Almsperson, by weekly or other periodical payments as the Trustees think fit, a stipend, being at the rate of 7s. 6d. a week in the case of single almspeople and 10s. a week in the case of a married couple."

It also introduced another category of benefits with

> "The payment of pensions by weekly or other periodical payments as the Trustees think fit, being at the rate of not less than 5 shillings a week and not more than 7 shillings a week."

The Scheme also specified that

> "The Almspeople and Pensioners shall be poor persons of good character who have resided in the Borough of Sutton Coldfield for not less than five years … who have not during that last two years received Poor Law relief, and who from age, ill-health, accident or infirmity, are wholly or in part unable to maintain themselves by their own exertions".

The Trustees could spend all or part of the pension for the benefit of the almsperson or pensioner and they could pay a lesser amount if the recipient had other income or assistance from relatives.

They decided to implement this part of the Scheme in August 1906, as far as funds allowed, and instructed the Clerk to advertise for applications. We are not told how many were received but in November of that year the Trustees agreed to pay fifteen pensions of five shillings. Pensions were renewed annually and the number and amounts were changed according to need and available funds. In November 1915, for example, they recorded that "having regard to the satisfactory state of the accounts … five more old age pensions be granted and that the Clerk issue advertisement and notices accordingly". A few months later the Trustees approved four new pensions and increased an existing one from two shillings and sixpence to five shillings. Soon after, they decided to "reduce the allowance to Thomas Stringer and his wife, inmates of the Hill almshouses, from ten shillings to seven shillings a week. This will enable Stringer to have his Old Age Pension increased from two shillings to five shillings a week". There are only occasional references to pensions in the minutes of Trustees' meetings but it is clear that they continued at 5 shillings a week and were in demand. In January 1931 nine people were selected from 39 applicants, making the total number of pensioners 28, and two years later 3 were successful out of 66 candidates. Three years after that there were 28 at 5 shillings and one at ten shillings and the payments continued until 1951 when the Trustees made reductions in most of their charitable expenditure.

No pensions were to be advertised until the total cost had been reduced to £5 per week, payments for blankets were pegged at £50, subscriptions to charitable institutions, like local hospitals, and for school clothing were reduced by half, Poor Maidens' Portions were suspended and the allowance to the Council for the Clerk's time was halved. According to a report from the Clerk which he wrote ten years later, these changes were because of "adverse balances on the eleemosynary account". Four months after the reductions it is noted that the death of three pensioners reduced weekly payments to £5. 15. 0. but by 1953, they were awarding pensions to new applicants again. The last reference to pensions occurs in June 1971 when there is a suggestion that the payments were being run down except for almshouse residents who were already receiving them.

From the beginning until the present day the provision of clothing for school children has been a major part of the Municipal Charities' support for local people. In 1894, "worsted school clothing (£16. 4. 0), girls' hats (£6. 6. 0), school caps and boots and shoes were provided" but there is no record of how the distribution took place. A new Scheme sealed by the Charity Commissioners in 1905 allowed clothing grants of up to a total of £165 for "children of deserving and necessitous persons resident in the borough.

A joint committee of members of the Borough Council and Trustees produced a report in 1907 setting out a method for administering clothing distribution. For each Ward there was to be a committee with a Chairman and Secretary and the money allocated, £330, was to be divided in proportion to the number of houses in the Ward. Notices inviting applications were posted and there were handbills for the schools. The previous practice of awarding materials was given up and complete garments were to be distributed by the members of the committees. They produced an application form for parents and an order form for local tradesmen and a circular was sent to parents to explain the system. From the 356 applications received 320 awards were made so that 624 children benefited at a cost of £296.

In 1909 another Scheme specified that the clothing grants were to be made to "poor children in the Borough of Sutton Coldfield who are in attendance at any Public Elementary School maintained by the Local Education Authority in the said Borough and have obtained from the Managers of the School a certificate of good conduct, regularity in attendance, and progress in learning". This Scheme again imposed a maximum of £165 on the clothing grants although that amount was being exceeded at the time and continued to be so.

Later that year we are told that each Ward clothing committee comprised fourteen members and a Chairman and the following allocations were approved:

Trinity	£40	Boldmere	£70
Maney	£70	Hill	£76
Wylde Green	£25	Walmley	£35

making a total of £316 out of the £330 available.

These committees, almost unchanged, continued the annual distribution of clothing and the amount of money remained the same until 1922 when the distribution of it was slightly changed so that Trinity Ward received £50, Hill, Walmley and Maney were the same, and Boldmere and Wylde Green were reduced by £5 each. The next change occurred in 1925 when each Ward received less and the total was reduced to £283 but no explanation is given. There were then no changes until 1934 when there were adjustments to the amounts allocated to the wards and the total increased to £307.

In May 1936 the Boldmere committee asked for an increase in their allocation which would be "based on equality" and they asked for 14 shillings for each application granted in the previous year. In response the Clerk collected statistics from the clothing committee secretaries and presented them to the Trustees in the table below.

SUMMARY OF RETURNS SUBMITTED BY WARD SECRETARIES
relating to awards of clothing for years 1930 to 1935 (inclusive).

Year	Ward	No. of Appns received.	No. of Appns granted.	No. of Appns refused.	Amount allocated By Trustees, £. s. d.	Average Award per case. £. s. d.
1930	Trinity	59	53	6	45.	17.
	Hill	137	106	31	68.	12. 10
	Boldmere	94	92	2	58.	12. 7
	Wylde Green	20	19	1	18.	18.
	Maney	92	72	20	63.	17. 6
	Walmley	56	45	11	31.	14.
1931	Trinity	48	47	1	45.	19.
	Hill	118	115	3	68.	11. 9
	Boldmere	104	100	4	58.	11. 7
	Wylde Green	22	19	3	18.	16. 4
	Maney	78	69	9	63.	18. 3
	Walmley	59	51	8	35.	13. 9
1932	Trinity	51	45	6	40.	18.
	Hill	134	112	22	68.	12. 1
	Boldmere	112	110	2	58.	10. 6
	Wylde Green	16	16	-	18.	1. 2. 4
	Maney	86	71	15	63.	17. 9
	Walmley	74	63	11	40.	12. 9
1933	Trinity	52	47	5	40.	17.
	Hill	142	127	15	68.	10. 8
	Boldmere	112	112	-	68.	12. 1
	Wylde Green	20	20	-	18.	18.
	Maney	78	67	11	63.	19.
	Walmley	86	66	20	40.	12. 1
1934	Trinity	49	41	8	40.	19. 6
	Hill	129	96	33	68.	14. 2
	Boldmere	106	104	2	68.	13.
	Wylde Green	21	21	-	18.	17. 2
	Maney	81	73	8	63.	17. 3
	Walmley	90	67	23	45.	13. 5
1935	Trinity	41	41	-	40.	19. 6
	Hill	117	96	21	68.	14. 2
	Boldmere	114	111	3	68.	12. 3
	Wylde Green	21	21	-	18.	17. 2
	Maney	82	78	4	63.	16. 2
	Walmley	80	72	8	45.	12. 6

This shows the considerable differences between the wards, both in the number of applications and the amounts awarded. The number of successful applications remained fairly constant in most of the wards but in Walmley there was an increase from 45 in 1930 to 72 in 1935. To further illustrate the differences the table below shows the averages number of children over the period of six years:

CLOTHING GRANTS – AVERAGE VALUES 1930-35

WARD	No. applying	Awarded	% awarded	Amount
Trinity	50	46	92	18s
Hill	130	109	84	12s
Boldmere	107	105	98	12s
Wylde Green	20	19	95	18s
Maney	83	71	85	18s
Walmley	73	61	83	13s

For applicants, the success rate varied from 98% in Boldmere down to 83% in Walmley but the biggest discrepancy was in the amounts awarded to each applicant. A child in Trinity Ward, for example, received an average of 18 shillings whereas one in Hill or Boldmere would have received only 12 shillings so the Boldmere committee was justified in asking for this to be considered.

The outcome of the discussions which followed was that the Trustees decided to base the allocations to committees on 14 shillings a head (slightly less for Walmley) which produced the following results:

Trinity	£38	14s	previous year	£40
Hill	£67	14s		£68
Boldmere	£77	14s		£68
Wylde Green	£14	14		£18
Maney	£54	12s		£63
Walmley	£49	14s		£45
Total	**£293**	**2s**		**£307**

So Boldmere and Walmley received small increases and the other wards received less whilst the cost to the charities was reduced. Although the figures for each year are not available it seems that the total amount allocated for clothing grants remained at £300 a year, despite inflation, until 1951 when it was reduced to £150.

In 1953 the number of applications from Trinity and Wylde Green was small so they were added to Boldmere and each of the four committees was then given up to £50 to spend on grants. In the following year the Clerk reported that although each committee had used its £50 the grants to each child varied from 9s 9d to £1 5s 2d so the Trustees decided to continue with £50 for each committee but to limit the amount for each child to a maximum of 10 shillings. However, a year later some grants over that limit were approved and the Trustees decided in 1957 that the award could be up to £1 per child. Four years later the Clerk produced a report which set out the history of the clothing grants and showed that in 1960 there had been 219 applications of which 205 were successful and the average award was 14 shillings per child. He recommended an increase in the total amount from £200 to £300 and suggested up to £5 per child and £10 per family. A child was defined as a person under 16. The Trustees accepted his recommendations and re-appointed the clothing committees. In the following year 252 grants were made, most of them in Walmley. There is no record of the number or size of grants for the next few years but the accounts for 1964 reveal that only £158 was spent on children's clothing and a surplus of £5,000 in the Educational Foundation was divided between the Council and the Secondary Education fund of the Charities. The amount allocated for clothing remained at £260 for most of the decade although the committees often exceeded this amount and the variation between wards was considerable if the figures recorded for 1967 are typical:

Boldmere and Banners Gate	£20
Hill	£25
Maney and Trinity	£15
Walmley	£200
Total	£260

In the following year the total was £307.

A new Scheme sealed in 1968 removed the limit on the total amount to be spent on school clothing and six months later the Trustees decided to continue to award up to £5 per child with a maximum of £10 per family with the result that expenditure for that year totalled £561. The system of Ward committee continued but their awards are not noted until 1971 when the amounts were:

Trinity and Maney	£25
Hill	£129
Boldmere and Wylde Green	£45
Walmley	£445

giving a total of £644. In the following year it was decided to increase the maximum awards to £7.50 per child and £15 per family so the total amount spent rose to £922.50 and a year after that, in 1973 the total rose to £1,097.50. Policy changes continued with the maximum for a family raised to £20 in 1974 and the committees being given executive power a year later when the total rose to £1,550.

In 1976 there was a cutback, for which no reasons are given, when the Trustees placed a maximum of £1,000 on the awards and also recommended that grants be given only to children at primary schools. How the Ward committees responded is not known but between then and 1983 the upper age limit was increased to 17 so, presumably, grants to secondary pupils continued in the period between. In 1979 the maximum per family was increased to £50, although the committee chairman had discretion to raise it further, and the proposed total of £4,000 was divided as follows:

Boldmere	£500
Maney	£500
Hill	£1,000
Walmley	£2,000

The family maximum was raised again to £60 in 1983 and the Trustees also decided to make awards for pupils up to the age of 18 instead of 17. It will be noted that the tables do not record any grants for pupils of secondary school age although they were being made. The committees had been re-formed and were awarded the following amounts:

Boldmere	£1,000
Hill	£3,000
Central	£1,000
Falcon Lodge	£4,000

With the family maximum increased to £75.

By 1987 the total for clothing grants had been increased again and in the following year they were raised again to:

Boldmere	£1,500
Hill	£3,000
Central	£3,000
Falcon Lodge	£8,000
Total	£15,500

Unfortunately, the basis for the changes is not recorded and committees sometimes exceeded their allocations so we do not know whether the increases were to meet a growth in the number of applications, rising costs or the decision of the Local Education Authority to discontinue its uniform grants.

In 1992-3 the new Clerk carried out an analysis of the clothing grants and the procedures and was concerned that parents were receiving different amounts in the four areas and that the grants did not appear to be related to actual costs. Schools were asked to provide their uniform requirements which were then costed so that an average amount for the special items of uniform could be calculated and it was then suggested that grants should be based on this amount. It was also proposed that the committees should be disbanded and the new formula applied by the permanent staff of the Charities. The Trustees agreed and the new system was introduced. Application forms were delivered to all schools in March and head teachers were asked to pass on information to parents and then collect the completed forms. When these were received at the Charities' office each one was considered in detail and the amount of the grant determined. As before no cash was distributed but parents were given vouchers to spend at the participating store of their choice. Any unusual cases were referred to the Chairman of the Trustees. The system worked well but it became clear from enquiries to some of the parents and stores that the amounts awarded were sometimes over generous and so they were adjusted in subsequent years. The cost of the scheme has varied from year to year so in 1995-6 1,244 children received vouchers worth a total of £74,075 but in 1999-2000 853 children received grants totalling £37,415 and there has been a steady decline in the in the number and total value of the grants since then.

An important category of grants now is personal awards to individuals in need but these are of relatively recent origin. There was one was in November, 1911 when Mr Jude Jones was given £2 to help him with the cost of visiting his daughter who was in hospital in Torquay and another in 1920 when £16 was given for an artificial arm for a girl of 16 but the next one was not until 1971 when two Scouts were given £30 each to help with the cost of their visit to the World Jamboree. Interestingly, there is a note in the minutes that an application for assistance with the purchase of a motorised wheelchair in 1948 was refused on the grounds that it was not within the scope of the scheme. Such assistance is now given quite frequently. In 1975 a grant of £50 was given to the Sutton Coldfield District Scouts Association towards the £560 cost of sending four Scouts to the World Jamboree. By 1991 grants to individuals were given quite frequently but they are not recorded in the general minutes, partly because of confidentiality. During the next decade the provision of such grants became a significant part of the support provided by the Charities and by 1996–7 awards to individuals ranged from £50 to £4,000 totalling over £52,000. In the remaining years of the twentieth century the totals were somewhat lower but the highest individual grant was £7,200 in 1997-8. Many of these grants were for essential domestic equipment, such as cookers, refrigerators and washing machines, but occasionally included awards for repairs, exemplified by help for a very elderly couple living in quite a large property in Wylde Green. Their plight only came to light when neighbours called in the public health department to investigate the presence of rats. The couple had a kitchen with a leaking roof, deficient heating arrangements and the house was in a generally poor condition. A grant from the Charities helped to improve their situation quickly and statutory bodies were alerted for longer term support.

Grants have been made to a variety of organisations which improve the lives of the residents and perhaps the most important category has been for their health. The first such awards was in 1908 when the Cottage Hospital opened and a grant of five guineas was made, to be followed, a year later, by the following: two guineas each to the Dental Hospital, the Ear, Nose and Throat Hospital and the Eye Hospital and five guineas to the Sutton Coldfield Dispensary. Except for the Dispensary the others were in Birmingham but the grants were presumably justified because the institutions served the people of Sutton Coldfield. These grants continued unchanged until 1913 when the Hahneman Convalescent Home in Bournemouth was added to enable "twelve weeks treatment at a nominal charge to be made for persons suffering from tubercular diseases." In 1918 there was another development when, in addition to the annual grants, the Trustees gave "Special Contributions" of 25 guineas to the Cottage Hospital and 15 guineas to the Sutton Coldfield Dispensary.

Two years later, they added the Sutton Coldfield Home of Rest to both lists with a grant of 5 guineas and a Special Contribution of 15 guineas and in 1921 they added a Special Contribution of 2 guineas for the district nurses of the Four Oaks and Hill Nursing Association and one of 10 guineas for the General Hospital in Birmingham with a future subscription of 3 guineas. The annual grants and the so-called special contributions were renewed each year until 1924 when no special contribution was made to the Eye Hospital or the General Hospital but they continued to receive an annual grant. The Royal Orthopaedic and Spinal Hospital and Blackwell Sanatorium were added to the list and remained on it until 1946 when the list comprised:

	Nursing Home and Cottage Hospital	5 guineas
	Sutton Coldfield Dispensary	5g
	Sutton Coldfield Home of Rest	5g
	Ear and Throat Hospital	2g
	Dental Hospital	3g
	Hill and Four Oaks Nursing Association	5g
	Birmingham and Midland Eye Hosp.	2g
	Birmingham General Hospital	10g
	Royal Orthopaedic and Spinal Hospital	3g
	Blackwell Sanatorium	5g
	Birmingham and Midland Skin Hosp.	3g
	Midland Nerve Hospital	2g
Special contributions	Sutton Coldfield Hospital	35g
	Sutton Coldfield Dispensary	20g
	Sutton Coldfield Home of Rest	10g
	Hill and Four Oaks Nursing Association	5g
	Sutton Coldfield Maternity Unit	£20

Note: A guinea was £1 and 1 shilling which is £1.05p in today's currency.

The introduction of the National Health Service in 1946 brought an end to most of these grants despite requests from some of the recipients for them to continue. In 1948, the Dispensary and Maternity Unit received £30 each and the Home of Rest and Hill and Four Oaks Nursing Association were given £20 each. The last two grants of this kind, which were awarded in 1948, were £45 to the Home of Rest and £55 to the Maternity Unit.

In 1985, the income of the Charities increased from £16,000 in the previous year to over £20,000 and unspent income amounted to a total of approaching £210,000. With this growth in income which continued towards the end of the century, the Trustees began to think about new ways of making grants and in 1985 they decided to make a "Major Award" of £100,000 which, for the first year, was to be for Youth Activities. Applicants were to submit proposals by September, the Grants Committee would compile a short list and the full Board would then decide on the successful bids. Applications totalling £218,281 were received from 23 organisations from which12 were selected for awards ranging from £250 to £10,000. The accounts for 1985-6 show that income increased by £102,000 to £501,000 and that the unspent income rose from £239,000 to £378,000. In 1986 the Major Award was for the benefit of unemployed people but it was less successful because there were very few organisations to represent this group. Also in that year it was decided to make a grant of £200,000 to Good Hope Hospital for a scanner and another £25,000 was added three months later so the previous very small annual grants were replaced by individual ones for specific purposes. In the following year the Major Award of £250,000 was designated for organisations serving elderly people and in 1988 £400,000 was set aside for health. There were nine grants ranging from £650 to £11,000 and another grant to Good Hope Hospital, this time of £155,000. However, these were not the only grants for the health and welfare of Sutton Coldfield residents since the totals for this category were £210,027 for 1987, £334,989 for 1988 and then £37,160 for 1989 when there was no Major Award.

In subsequent years grants were not categorised in the same way but an examination of the Annual Reports shows that, in addition to many smaller amounts, some large sums of money were distributed to organisations concerned with health and special needs. For example:

1995/6	Handicapped Children and Adults Association (now the Norman Laud Association) for a respite care home for adults	
		£100,000
1997/8	Marie Curie Cancer Care Nurses	£20,000
	Good Hope Hosp. bronchoscopy equipment	£24,474
	Cottage Hospital	£7,046
	Greenacres Cheshire Home new unit	£200,000
	St Giles Hospice lymphoedema clinic	£50,000

	Acorns Children's' Hospice	£30,000
	Norman Laud Association rent	£11,500
1998/9	Fellowship of the Handicapped minibus	£21,000
	Norman Laud Association rent	£11,500
	Norman Laud Association charity shop set-up	£56,000
	City of Birmingham Special Olympics expenses	£10,000
1999/2000	KIDS for decoration and refurbishment	£10,000
	Norman Laud Association for rent	£16,000
	Sutton Special Olympics for minibus	£15,000
	Good Hope Hospital for equipment	£12,300
	Good Hope Hospital for X-ray equipment	£600,000

Although it was after the period covered here it is interesting to note that the largest ever grant in this category was made in 2006 when an award of £1.33 million was made to St Giles Hospice for a day care centre to support their work for patients in Sutton Coldfield. This was built on land belonging to the Charities and formerly occupied by Barn Farm which had become derelict.

Except for the Major Awards the Trustees have largely been reactive in their grant making and in the last decade of the twentieth century more and more local organisations like schools, churches, amateur sport and drama groups had become aware that they could apply for financial assistance. From 1987 to 1991 the total amount given in grants varied a little from year to year but was in the region of £400,000 to almost £500,000 but in 1992 it rose to over £845,000 and a year later the total was £1,357,163. In the following years the total varied between £748,042 in 1996-6 and £1,759,294 in 1998-9 but was over £1 million from 1996 to 2000. To some extent the increase in expenditure was the result of some suggestions from the Charity Commissioners about the proper use of income and their concern that some of it was not being used.

Schools in Sutton Coldfield became major beneficiaries from 1987, when they were given £35,217 and increasing amounts for the next thirteen years. In 1989 schools were given a total of almost £63,000 and at this time many requests were for minibuses. One reason for the larger grants was the increased sums of money available but another was the re-interpretation of paragraph 31(1) in the Scheme of 1982. Writing about the "application of income for the advancement of education" this section states it may be used for:

"providing such special benefits of any kind *not normally provided by the local education authority* for any school in the area of benefit … as shall from time to time be agreed between the school governors or managers and the Trustees after consultation with the local education authority"

Hitherto this paragraph had been interpreted fairly strictly and grants had been made for hall curtains, library books and minibuses, for example. With limited local authority funds available grants began to be made when the local authority could not pay or did not choose to pay and schools were awarded grants for such things as computer equipment and library refurbishment.

In 1996-7 three of the secondary schools received large amounts for library development (£111,000 to Sutton Girls School, £106,207 to Arthur Terry School and £50,000 to Fairfax School). In the following year the grants to primary schools included £16,000 to St Joseph's and £10,000 to Hollyfield Juniors for library improvements and £17,000 to Boldmere Juniors for computing equipment. At this time the amounts awarded were based upon the needs expressed by the school and the number of pupils but by 1999 changes in educational finance brought new developments. Secondary schools were able to apply for specialist college status which brought significant financial benefits if they were able to raise a prescribed sum of money from other sources such as local businesses or, in Sutton Coldfield, the Municipal Charities. Not all the requests were for that purpose but those that were set a high baseline for grants as shown in the table below for secondary schools:

YEAR	SCHOOL	AMOUNT	PURPOSE
1998-9	Arthur Terry	£94,500	Info. Tech. equipment
	Fairfax	£90,000	Assembly Hall Extension
	Sutton Girls	£98,000	Food Technology, Tennis courts
	Plantsbrook	£90,300	Science provision
	Bishop Vesey's	£75,000	Sports Hall
1999-2000	Bishop Walsh	£74,639	Performing Arts equipment
	John Willmott	£100,000	Library and IT equipment
	Bishop Vesey's	£75,000	Extension to Sports Hall

During the same period many grants were also made to the primary school as shown by the examples in the table:

YEAR	SCHOOL	AMOUNT	PURPOSE
1998-99	Newhall Jun. & Infant	£13,000	Computer equipment
	Four Oaks Juniors	£18,817	Library refurbishment
	Town Juniors	£3,200	Science room alterations
	Moor Hall Juniors	£18,555	Computer equipment & library
	Little Sutton Primary	£20,00	Computer suite
	Penns Primary	£20,000	Computer suite
	Holland House Infants	£9,000	Play area & kitchen.
	Boldmere Infants	£23,000	Play area & fencing
	Banners Gate Infants	£11,570	Play area
	Walmley Infants	£18,000	Classroom equipment
1999-2000	Banners Gate Juniors	£5,000	Display panels
	Minworth Jun, & Inf.	£8,500	Computer equipment
	Holy Cross	£17,900	Computer suite
	Holy Cross	£10,000	Floor tiling
	St Nicholas	£15,000	External play equipment
	Whitehouse Common	£20,000	Refurb. Of Science and Craft Unit
	Mere Green Primary	£20,000	Computer equipment
	Deanery Primary	£9,300	Computer equipment
	Walmley Juniors	£15,000	Computer equipment
	New Oscott Infants	£10,310	Computer equipment

These grants enabled the schools to respond more quickly to curriculum developments such as the increasing use of computers and to provide other facilities which they may not have been able to afford so soon, if at all, from official funds or parental fundraising.

A variety of local groups which support, entertain and provide for the well-being of local residents of all ages have received support as an examination of the list of grants published each year makes clear. Elderly people who attend clubs which meet regularly or who live in special accommodation have received grants to help with Christmas celebrations and summer outings. Societies, which put on performances of plays or musicals and choirs and orchestras which can rarely raise the necessary funds from ticket sales and other activities have been supported by grants towards their expenses. Many sports clubs have received awards to help with maintenance of buildings, courts and other facilities or for special events.

Most of the churches within the area of benefit have received awards to help with both worship and other activities and for a diversity of purposes such building extensions or additional buildings, for music, for improving facilities, especially kitchens and heating, and, occasionally, for specific events or staff costs.

The following list of grants made from 1997 to 2000 will illustrate the variety and scale of such grants at the end of the century.

Falcon Lodge Chapel – minibus	£10,000
Boldmere Methodist Refurbishment of Community area	£12,260
United Reformed Church – Kitchen and disabled toilet	£20,000
St Peter's – drainage work	£44,000
St Nicholas RC refurbishment	£28,000
Emmanuel – Refurbishment of church building	£28,000
Four Oaks Baptist – Extension and improvements	£50,000
Sacred Heart RC refurbishment of church hall	£50,000
Emmanuel Church – new organ	£94,000
Central Churches Trust – Carpenters Arms*	£171,000
Four Oaks Methodist – heating/building work	£68,000
Sutton Coldfield. Methodist – electrical work	£17,500
Holy Cross for floor tiling	£10,000

* This group of churches, which had provided community activities based in the old library in the centre of Sutton Coldfield, was forced to move when the building was sold for redevelopment. They found a new base in a former church hall in Boldmere but it required extensive building work and repairs before it could be used for community activities. Because of the Trust's Christian basis it was named "The Carpenter's Arms".

All group applicants for grants were required to explain the purpose, and scale of the project and the number of people who would benefit from it. They were also asked to give costs and the amount of money available from their own funds, supported by a recent set of accounts. The Clerk to the Trustees or another officer of the Charities would normally make a visit to meet representatives and discuss the project before the application was submitted to the Board or the Grants sub-committee which would be provided with a full written report and information about previous grants.

Finally, the scale of the support now given to the residents of Sutton Coldfield in the various ways described above may be illustrated by the total sums of money awarded in the final decade of the century:

TOTAL EXPENDITURE ON GRANTS

1989	1990	1991	1992	1993	
455,764	459,965	492,832	845,064	1,357,163	

1994	1995	1996	1997	1998	1999
901,561	867,023	1,086,628	1,014,904	1,759,294	1,505,961

From an annual expenditure of about £40 to purchase clothing for children not only has the amount of money increased hugely but much of the grant-making has moved on from providing basic necessities to improving the quality of life through education and leisure activities. Whilst individual applicants have to provide evidence of income so that only the relatively needy benefit from grants, many others, whatever their financial situation, who belong to leisure organisations also receive help indirectly through their membership. The residents of Sutton Coldfield are fortunate to have such a source of individual and group support from the Charities the sound management of which has produced such a significant growth in resources.

REFERENCES

An Impartial Hand   The History of Sutton Coldfield, London, 1762

Bedford, Rev.W.K Riland   Three Hundred Years of Family Living, Cornish
                           Brothers, 1889

Bedford, Rev.W.K Riland   A History of Sutton Coldfield, 1891.

Bracken, Miss   A History of the Forest and Chase of Sutton
                           Coldfield, London, Simpkin, Marshall and
                           Co, c.1860

Jones, Douglas, V   The Royal Town of Sutton Coldfield, Sutton
                           Coldfield Corporation, 1973

Jones, Douglas, V   Sutton Park, Westwood Press, 1982

Lea, Roger   The Story of Sutton Coldfield, Stroud, Sutton
                           Publishing, 2003

Lea, Roger   Scenes From Sutton's Past, Westwood Press,
                           1989

Midgley, A   A Short History of the Town and Chase of
                           Sutton Coldfield, The Midland Counties
                           Herald Ltd, 1904

Osbourne, Kerry   A History of Bishop Vesey's Grammar School,
                           Rosemary Wilkinson, Sutton Coldfield, 1990.

Reay-Nadin, R.A   Sutton Coldfield, Health Resorts Association,
                           1913

Redwood, D   The Origins of the Elementary School System in
                           Sutton Coldfield, in Scenes from Suttons Past,
                           Lea

Various authors   The Royal Town of Sutton Coldfield,
                           Corporation, 1951

Victoria History of the County of Warwick, vol. IV, Oxford University Press,
1904 and 1947.

Minutes of Meetings of Sutton Coldfield Municipal Charities – Stored in
Sutton Coldfield Reference Library.